Kiddiwalks

IN
WILTSHIRE

Nigel Vile

COUNTRYSIDE BOOKS
NEWBURY BERKSHIRE

First published 2010
© Nigel Vile 2010

COUNTRYSIDE BOOKS
3 Catherine Road
Newbury, Berkshire

To view our complete range of books,
please visit us at
www.countrysidebooks.co.uk

ISBN 978 1 84674 179 1

Designed by Peter Davies, Nautilus Design
Produced through MRM Associates Ltd., Reading
Typeset by Jean Cussons Typesetting, Diss, Norfolk
Printed in Thailand

Contents

AREA MAP SHOWING LOCATION OF THE WALKS

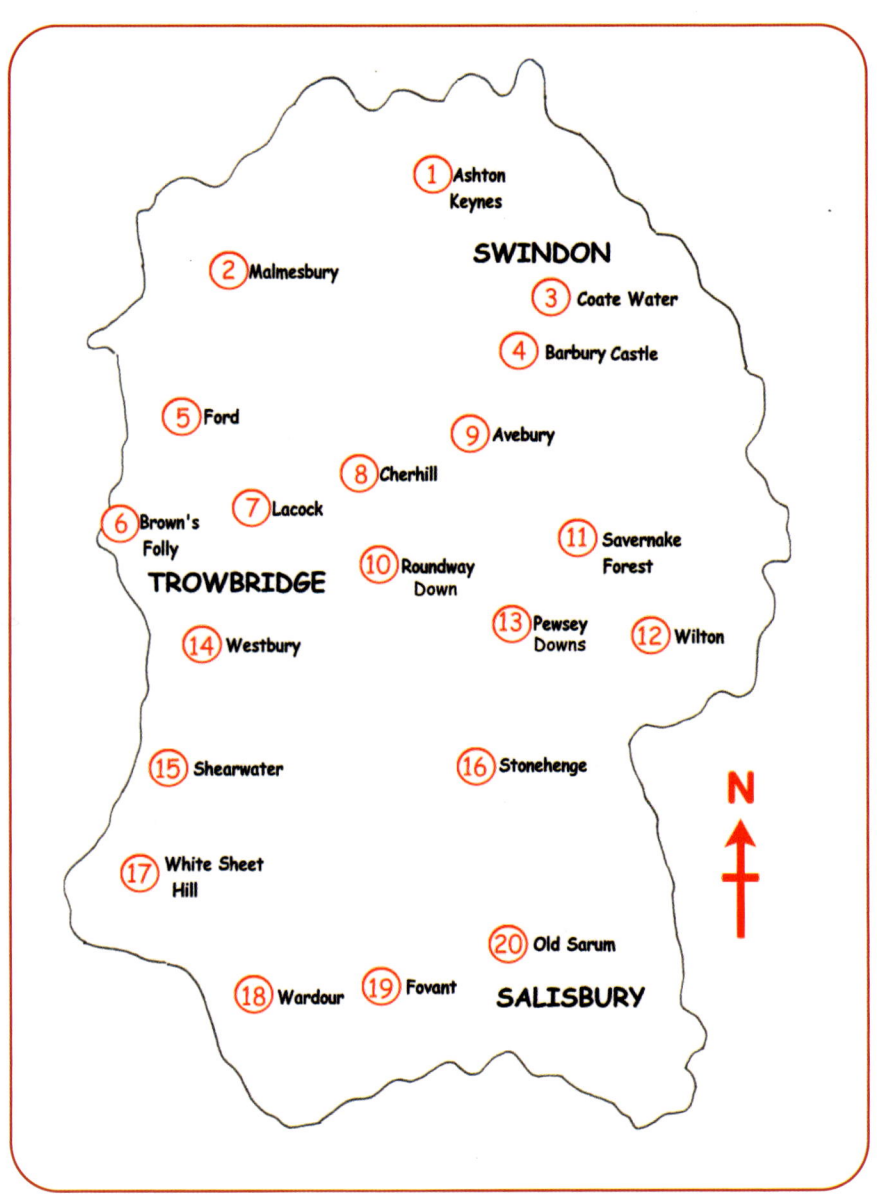

1. Ashton Keynes

SWINDON

2. Malmesbury

3. Coate Water

4. Barbury Castle

5. Ford

9. Avebury

8. Cherhill

7. Lacock

6. Brown's Folly

TROWBRIDGE

10. Roundway Down

11. Savernake Forest

13. Pewsey Downs

12. Wilton

14. Westbury

15. Shearwater

16. Stonehenge

N

17. White Sheet Hill

20. Old Sarum

18. Wardour

19. Fovant

SALISBURY

Contents

PUBLISHER'S NOTE

We hope that you obtain considerable enjoyment from this book; great care has been taken in its preparation. Although at the time of publication all routes followed public rights of way or permitted paths, diversion orders can be made and permissions withdrawn.

We cannot, of course, be held responsible for such diversion orders and any inaccuracies in the text which result from these or any other changes to the routes nor any damage which might result from walkers trespassing on private property. We are anxious though that all details covering the walks are kept up to date and would therefore welcome information from readers which would be relevant to future editions.

The simple sketch maps that accompany the walks in this book are based on notes made by the author whilst checking out the routes on the ground. They are designed to show you how to reach the start, to point out the main features of the overall circuit and they contain a progression of numbers that relate to the paragraphs of the text.

However, for the benefit of a proper map, we do recommend that you purchase the relevant Ordnance Survey sheet covering your walk. The Ordnance Survey maps are widely available, especially through booksellers and local newsagents.

Introduction

Being a writer of walking guidebooks, I am often asked for advice or recommendations for routes. Friends with young children have a particular set of requirements. 'It must be a short walk, not too many hills and with something to interest the children along the way.' There is usually a footnote, too, that the walk must have a family-friendly pub or teashop, as much for the adults as the children!

The emphasis in this book of 'Kiddiwalks' matches the above specification almost perfectly. The objective is to provide relatively short and undemanding walks with a variety of attractions to stimulate the interest of children. It may be the ever-popular stream or river, it could be a long barrow or hillfort, possibly a cave or safe rock scramble. With distances that range between 1 and 3 miles, there are routes here that will suit everyone from toddlers to top juniors, as well as their parents and grandparents.

I have lived in Wiltshire for over 30 years. As a teacher, I regularly took parties of pupils onto the county's downlands, where we would explore hillforts and other ancient ruins, as well as discover the rich flora and fauna that has its home on this unique habitat. This is also the area where my own children spent much of their formative years exploring the countryside.

Each walk is presented in as user-friendly a manner as possible. There is firstly an outline of the route, emphasising in particular the features that youngsters will find most interesting. This is followed by a 'fact file' recording all of the key information such as the distance and timing for the walk, how to get to the start point and refreshment facilities. The nature of the terrain is also indicated, enabling you to decide if a particular walk is suitable for your family. As well as the walk directions and a map, there are details of the places and sights along the way, including a special 'Fun Things to See and Do ' section for children.

These walks were some of my own children's favourites in their early years, and I am sure that it was these short routes with their 'child-friendly' attractions that instilled in them a love of the great outdoors. I commend these walks to you.

Nigel Vile

1

Ashton Keynes and the Cotswold Water Park

A Lakeland Paradise

One of the many lakes at the water park.

T he Cotswold Water Park is Britain's largest and consists of over 140
lakes created by gravel extraction. Covering more than 40 square
miles – an area 50% larger than the Norfolk Broads – the park is
growing each year as gravel extraction evolves in the area. As its website
boasts: 'Whether you are a walker, birdwatcher, photographer, angler,
outdoor enthusiast or a family, there's sure to be something for you!' As
if all of this water was not enough, the infant River Thames makes a
fleeting appearance in the picturesque village of Ashton Keynes – and if
you are there in springtime, you will find the riverbank awash with
daffodils.

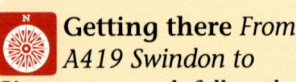

Getting there *From the A419 Swindon to Cirencester road, follow the Water Park's Spine Road. In 3 miles, turn left into Ashton Keynes on the B4696. In just ½ mile, park on the left by the church.*

Length of walk 2 miles.
Time 2 hours.
Terrain A flat and easy walk. Be prepared for a few muddy sections following heavy rainfall.
Start/Parking Alongside Ashton Keynes church (GR 042944).
Map OS Explorer 169 Cirencester & Swindon.

Refreshments The Horse and Jockey in Ashton Keynes is a family-friendly pub. There is an attractive garden that is especially suitable for children.

1 Walk through the churchyard to a handgate, before following a footpath for 200 yards to reach the Thames. Do not cross, but walk to the left – alongside the river – and continue past a rank of cottages to reach a road. Turn left and follow this road – Cox's Hill – for 350 yards up to the B4696. Turn left and, in just 20 yards, cross a stile on the right-hand side of the road.

The Walk

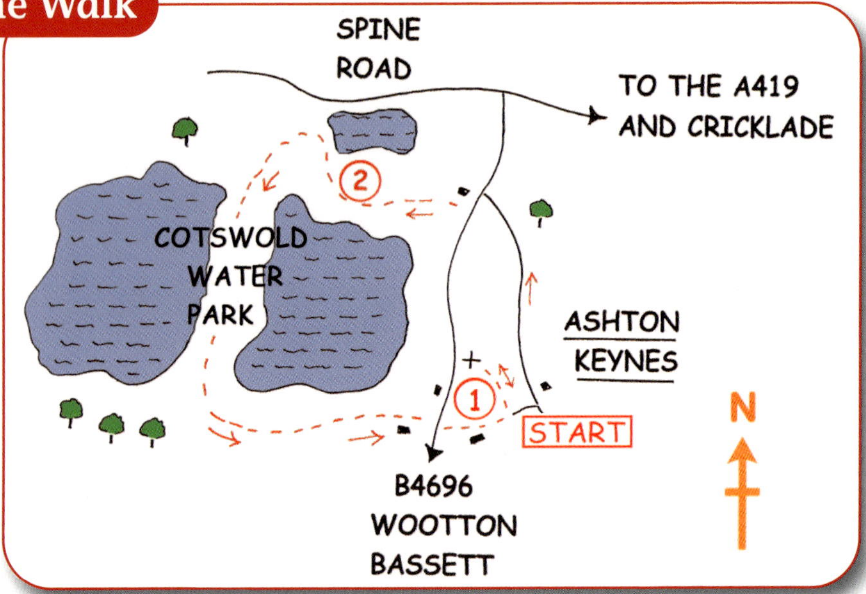

SPINE ROAD

TO THE A419 AND CRICKLADE

COTSWOLD WATER PARK

②

ASHTON KEYNES

①

START

N

B4696 WOOTTON BASSETT

Ashton Keynes and the Cotswold Water Park

The infant River Thames at Ashton Keynes.

Follow an enclosed path running between a hedge and an open field along to a stile. Beyond this stile, bear half-left to a stile in a fence on the left before walking ahead across the next field to a stile in front of some trees opposite. Continue along a path to a gravelled road.

2 Follow this road around to the right to a junction, before bearing left to walk between a pair of lakes. In 150 yards, keep on the track as it bears sharply left to follow a narrow strip of land running between another pair of lakes. In 800 yards, on approaching the end of the lake on the left, bear left and follow the lake's southern shoreline across to a prominent old building – a manor house – some 600 yards distant. Beyond a gate, continue on the path that passes to the left of this manor house along to the B4696. Turn right for a few paces, cross the Thames and immediately turn left along the Thames Path. In 250 yards, just past a property on the left, cross the Thames and follow the path on the left back up to Ashton Keynes church.

◆ Fun Things to See and Do ◆

The lakes that make up the Cotswold Water Park have become a **haven for wildfowl** and children will enjoy some bird spotting. This is Wiltshire's most important wetland site and it provides many of the county's wader and duck records. Over 200 bird species have been recorded. Coot can number about 6,000 whilst pochard exceed 3,000. The all year round residents include grey heron and Canada goose, kingfisher and dipper, whilst seasonal visitors can include Bewick's swan and greenshank, sand martin and dunlin. A guidebook to birds is a must on this walk, as is a pair of binoculars and a lot of patience!

◆ Background Notes ◆

The **Cotswold Water Park** is an area of lakes in the North Wiltshire and South Gloucestershire part of the Upper Thames catchment area. The lakes have been created from decades of sand and gravel extraction. Set to continue for many more years, this activity will result in the creation of further lakes in the future. The Water Park is nationally important for wildlife, supporting large numbers of wintering wildfowl, including winter populations of pochard, gadwell, coot and great crested grebe. Many of the lakes are Sites of Special Scientific Interest on account of their aquatic plants; the area also supports otters, water voles and the native white-clawed crayfish.

Writing in 1826 in his *Rural Rides*, William Cobbett recorded that 'I had to go through a village called Ashton Keines with which place I was very much smitten. It is now a straggling village but to a certainty it has been a large Market Town. There is a Market Cross still standing in an open space in it and there are such numerous lanes, crossing each other and cutting the land into such little bits that it must at one time have been a large Town.' Many years later, Arthur Mee was equally taken with this delightful village. He wrote: 'The shallow Isis flows past its charming stone cottages, spanned by little bridges leading to their gardens. There are three simple old crosses in the village and another by the church, to which an avenue of splendid elms brings us across to the church.' It is a pretty place, so much so that Humphrey Pakington in his *England's Villages and Hamlets*, published in 1941, included **Ashton Keynes** in his fifteen best villages … despite his disappointment at an incongruously placed pair of telegraph poles!

The **River Thames** is the longest river in England, some 215 miles long as it runs from Thames Head in Gloucestershire into the heart of London. Other statistics are equally impressive – it has a catchment area of some 5,000 square miles whilst 38 main tributaries feed the river between its source and its tidal limit at Teddington Lock. The diminutive river that flows through the village of Ashton Keynes will seem a million miles from the great river that forms such a well-known landmark in the capital, but hereabouts the line from *Prothalamion* by Edmund Spenser will certainly ring true, 'Sweet Thames! run softly, till I end my song'.

2

Malmesbury and the River Avon

Step Back in Time

Malmesbury's fine abbey.

There is no doubting that Malmesbury is a place of great antiquity. As you approach the town, the signs point out to all and sundry that this is 'England's Oldest Borough', a fact confirmed by the magnificent outline of the abbey that dominates the skyline. The actual Royal Charter conferring borough status was granted by Alfred the Great back in AD 880. The town itself sits upon a hilltop overlooking two branches of the River Avon, which meet here – the Sherston and Tetbury branches. This quite delightful little walk gives every opportunity to discover the heart of Malmesbury, as well as exploring the meadows that border the Avon on its fringes. Altogether it's a marvellous excuse to visit one of England's finest small towns.

Kiddiwalks in Wiltshire

2

Length of walk 2 miles.
Time 2 hours.
Terrain A flat and easy walk. There may be a few muddy sections alongside the river following heavy rainfall.
Start/Parking The pay & display long-stay Old Station car park below Malmesbury Abbey alongside the River Avon (GR 933875).
Map OS Explorer 168 Stroud, Tetbury & Malmesbury.
Refreshments There are many pubs and cafés in Malmesbury. A particular favourite is Amanda's Tea Shop in Oxford Street.

1 Walk to the end of the car park and follow a path on the right that crosses the Avon, signposted to the town centre. At a junction, climb some steps and follow a path to the left that passes the abbey to emerge onto a back lane. Walk along this lane to a square by the market cross. Walk right across this square, passing the entrance to the abbey, and follow Birdcage Walk down to the busy B4040. Cross to a pavement opposite, turn left and walk along to a left-hand bend. On this bend, turn right down a tarmac footpath, continuing down some steps to a junction. Turn right down a path called Burnivale. At the bottom of this path, follow a footpath on the left down to some bridges over the river. Continue to a diminutive stone clapper bridge before bearing left to a gap at the left-hand end of a stone wall. Follow the left edges of the next two fields to a handgate and join the banks of the River Avon. Follow the riverside path along to a handgate, turn left and cross a footbridge over the Avon by Avon Mills and continue along to the main B4014.

2 Turn left for a few paces and then right by the Rose and Crown pub into St John's Street. Walk along this back road for 200 yards and, immediately past the local bowls club and its green, turn left onto a footpath. Cross a footbridge and a stile and enter an open field. Walk across to a stile at the end of the field before crossing a second field to a stile and the B4040. Turn right, cross the Avon and immediately left onto a riverside path that borders the car park of an Indian restaurant. Beyond a gate, follow the riverside path through the Conygre Mead Nature Reserve to an exit gate just before the car park.

Beside the River Avon.

2

The Walk

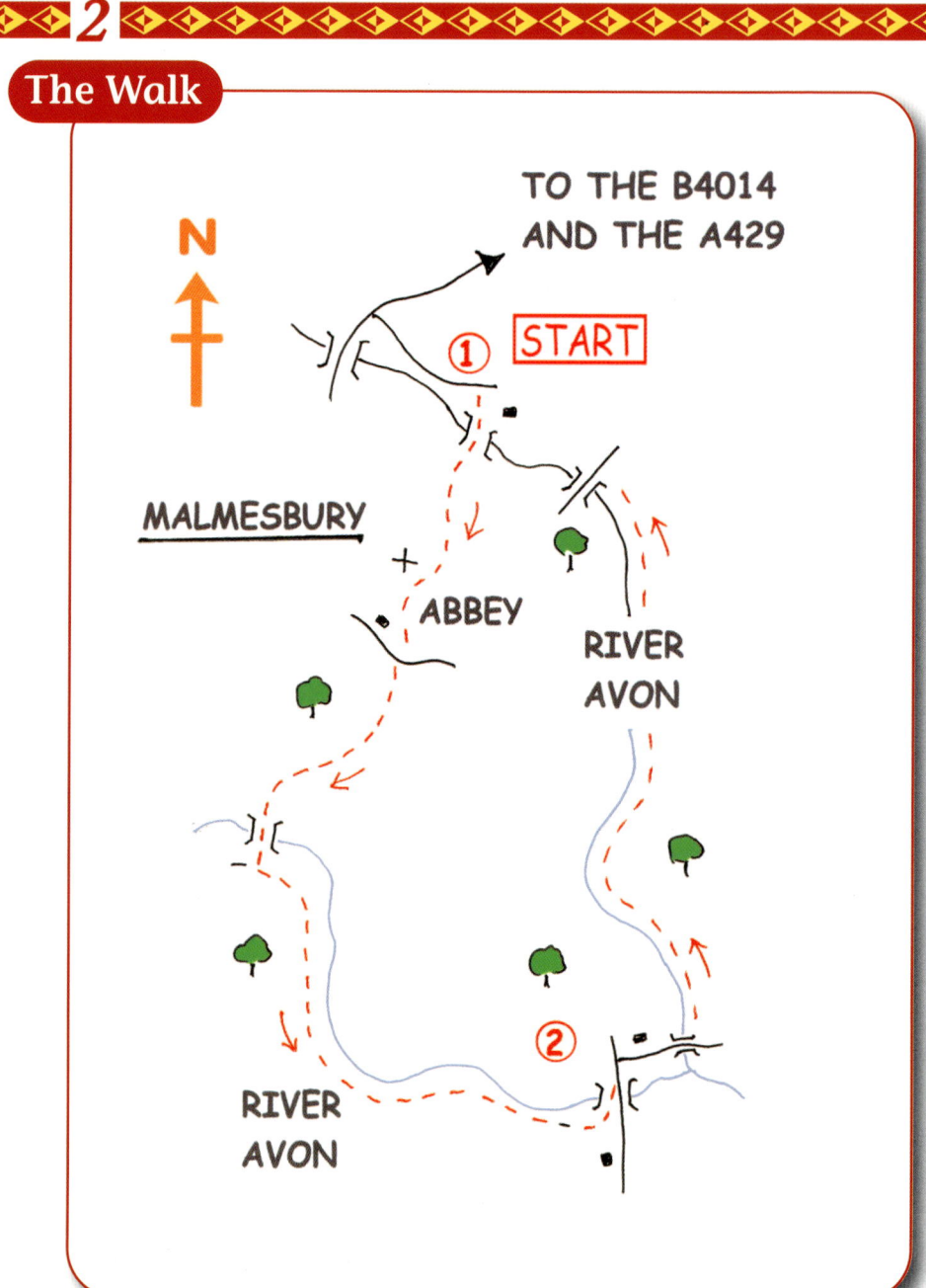

TO THE B4014
AND THE A429

N

① START

MALMESBURY

ABBEY

RIVER
AVON

②

RIVER
AVON

Malmesbury and the River Avon

◆ Fun Things to See and Do ◆

 Churchyards are full of **interesting old tombs and gravestones**. The churchyard at Malmesbury Abbey is no exception. See if you can find the grave of Hannah Twynnoy who, in the 18th century, laid claim to a dubious honour – the first person on record to be eaten by a tiger in Britain. This local barmaid was thrilled by the arrival of a travelling circus, but ignored warnings against teasing the menagerie's tiger. It broke free and mauled her to death. Inside the abbey, look for a stained-glass window dedicated to **Elmer the flying monk**. He had observed how jackdaws would circle the area, swooping and gliding, and decided to use the air currents and build himself wings, the material of which is not known. Fixing the wings to his wrists and flapping them as a bird would, he leapt from the abbey tower; he successfully travelled 200 yards before panic set in and he crashed to the ground, breaking both legs.

The walk passes through the **Conygre Mead Nature Reserve**. The word 'conygre' means 'where rabbits live'. Before the Reformation, the monks at Malmesbury Abbey used this area as a food source – principally for rabbit breeding – whilst ponds adjacent to the River Avon were used for stocking fish. There is plenty for children to look for in the reserve, which consists of grassland, a pond and woodland, and it is rich in flora and fauna. Plants include lady's bedstraw and field crane, water mint and yellow water lily. The rare sawfly *Macrophya albipuncta* occurs here, as well as the very occasional water vole. Grass snakes and slowworms have also been recorded.

Much of the walk follows two branches of the River Avon. **Water is always appealing to children** and, given the proximity of an accessible and shallow flow, be sure to bring a fishing net as the river is full of small fish such as minnows and sticklebacks.

◆ Background Notes ◆

Malmesbury can claim history at every corner, for here we have England's oldest borough, having been granted a charter by Alfred the Great. The first **abbey** was founded here by St Adhelm in the 7th century, although today's building dates mainly from the 12th century. Restoration work in the 14th century saw the addition of a rather grand tower, some 445 ft in height, but when it collapsed a century later much of the eastern end of the church was destroyed. The guidebooks point out the magnificent 12th-century carved porch, the tomb of King Ethelstan – the first Saxon king to rule the whole of England – and a puzzling watching loft on the south wall.

From the shadow of the abbey, this walk follows what is known as the '**Malmesbury Civic Trust River Walk**'. The town marks the confluence of two streams that both claim to be the River Avon, one flowing in from near Tetbury, the other from above Sherston; together they flow downstream through Bath and Bristol to the Bristol Channel at Avonmouth The first section of the walk follows the '**Sherston Branch**' across the watermeadows. This stretch of the walk brings with it fine views of the town, with its ranks of cottages and houses rising above the river towards the prominent abbey. Close to a stone slab bridge lies Daniel's Well, named after an early abbot who used to immerse himself up to his shoulders in this spot – come frost, wind or rain – in order to 'reduce the force of his rebellious body'.

The walk then follows the '**Tetbury Branch**' through the Conygre Mead Nature Reserve – at one time the monastery's rabbit warren – to Longmead and Tom Rich's Field, named after a farmer who had a butcher's shop in the town in the 1930s. Alongside the Conygre Mead Reserve, the exotic gardens bordering the river are the **Abbey House Gardens**, perhaps best known for being run by a pair of naked gardeners! Have no fears, Ian and Barbara Pollard, the owners, are not usually 'au nature' when the visiting public are admitted!

3

Coate Water

Don't Forget the Binoculars!

Scenic Coate Water.

A t first glance, the southern fringes of Swindon – the largest settlement in Wiltshire and, allegedly, one of the fastest growing towns within Europe – might appear fairly unpromising for a walk in the great outdoors. However, head down a quiet road off a busy roundabout and you will find yourself on the banks of Coate Water. This 72-acre lake with woodland fringes has well-constructed and level paths bordering the water's edge, making this the perfect walk for all ages.

Kiddiwalks in Wiltshire

3

Getting there *The Coate Water roundabout lies on the A4259, midway between Swindon town centre and junction 15 of the M4 motorway. A signposted turning runs from the roundabout to the car park.*

Length of walk 2 miles.
Time 2 hours.
Terrain A flat and easy walk around Coate Water. Occasionally there is mud in the woodland at the southern end of the lake.
Start/Parking Coate Water pay & display car park (GR 176827).

Map OS Explorer 169 Cirencester & Swindon.
Refreshments There is a café at the entrance to Coate Water that sells soft drinks and snacks.

1 From the car park, follow the footpath to the right up to Coate Water – the path is signposted to the café and toilets. At the top of the path, turn right and follow the right-hand side of the lake along to a kiosk for a golf course. Pass this kiosk and continue following a woodland path, with Coate Water beyond the bushes and trees on the left. On reaching a wooden barrier

◆ Fun Things to See and Do ◆

Being **a fine area for birdlife**, a spotter's guide and binoculars will be a must on this particular walk. A number of hides located around Coate Water will enable you to watch the wildlife without too much disturbance to their behavioural patterns. If you want to discover more about the lake and its wildlife, visit the **Ranger Centre** by the car park. Here an exhibition room houses a permanent display on Coate Water and its history dating back to the 1800s.

Around the lake are a number of attractions that will certainly appeal to youngsters of all ages. These include a **play area**, **a crazy golf course and a paddling pool**. Be sure to pack a towel and some spare clothes – or be prepared to travel home feeling very damp!

The Walk

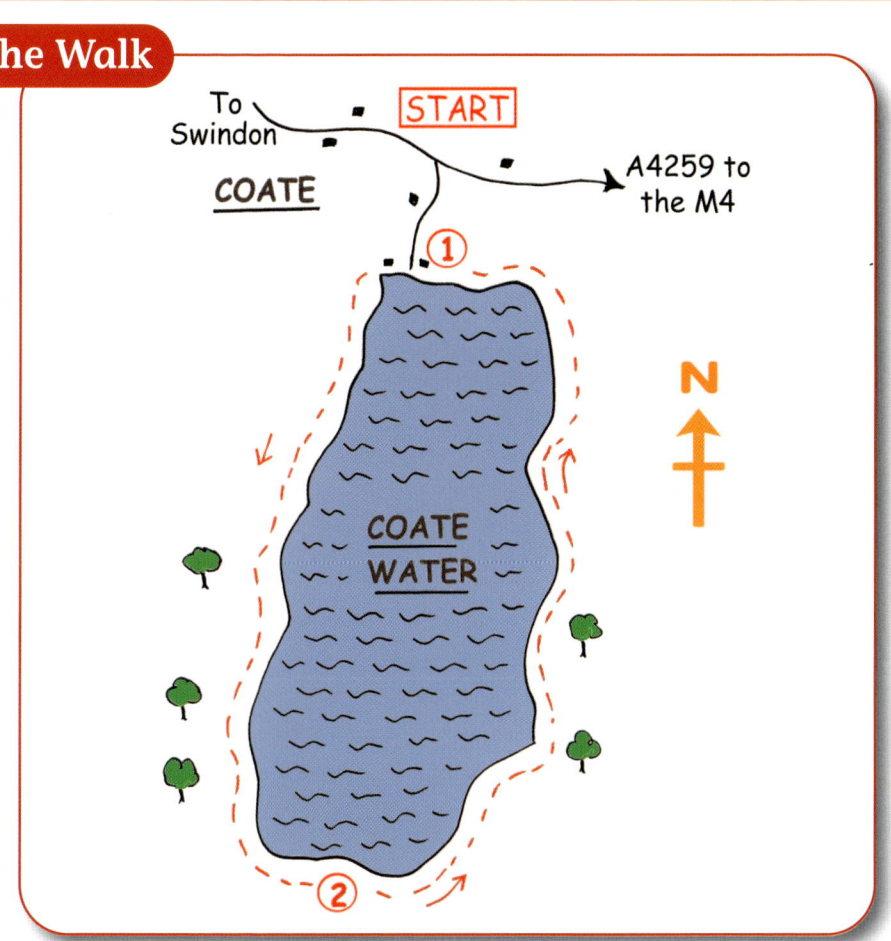

just before a road, turn left and follow a path along the southern end of Coate Water.

2 In 200 yards, turn left over a wooden footbridge and continue following a woodland path for ¼ mile to a junction. Turn left, and cross a bridge running between two lakes. At the junction just beyond this bridge, turn left to follow the path running alongside the water. Follow this path past a children's play area before bearing left along the northern edge of the lake back to the café. Turn right down to the car park.

Kiddiwalks in Wiltshire

In and out the tree trunks!

◆ Background Notes ◆

This short walk explores Coate Water, a man-made lake that was created as a reservoir for the Wiltshire and Berkshire Canal. Richard Jefferies, Wiltshire's best-known country writer, was born in Coate in 1848. He described this stretch of water as a 'weedy mere' – a great injustice to the magnificent country park that has subsequently been created! As you follow the lakeside walk, look out for the rich variety of birdlife that thrives both on the water and in the woodland bordering the shoreline. Great-crested grebes, grey herons, Canada geese, kingfishers, coots, little owls and lesser-spotted woodpeckers are but a selection of the species that can be seen here throughout the year.

Barbury Castle

Castle of Adventure

Walking on the ramparts.

E very major town has its 'playground' and the Barbury Castle Country Park fulfils this role for the expanding community of Swindon. Located high on the Marlborough Downs, with fine views in all directions and plenty of places for the children to run and climb, the walk includes a section of the Ridgeway. Arguably the country's oldest road, this ancient highway has been used by travellers, herdsmen and soldiers since pre-historic times. The Country Park, incidentally, takes its name from an Iron Age hillfort that enjoyed an unrivalled defensive location.

Kiddiwalks in Wiltshire

4

Getting there *Barbury Castle is reached from the B4005 south of Swindon. Approaching from junction 15 – Swindon East – on the M4 motorway, follow the A346 south to Chiseldon. Turn right onto the B4005 and follow the clearly signposted route to Barbury Castle.*

Length of walk 2 miles.
Time 2 hours.
Terrain A relatively flat and easy walk with just one gentle climb onto Barbury Castle.

Start/Parking Barbury Castle Country Park free car park (GR 157761).
Map OS Explorer 169 Cirencester & Swindon.
Refreshments Playing around on such lofty hilltops will certainly induce a healthy appetite. Barbury Farm – alongside the car park – has a café offering a wide range of drinks and snacks that can be enjoyed on picnic tables in a garden setting. Alternatively, you could bring along your own picnic to enjoy in the great outdoors.

The Walk

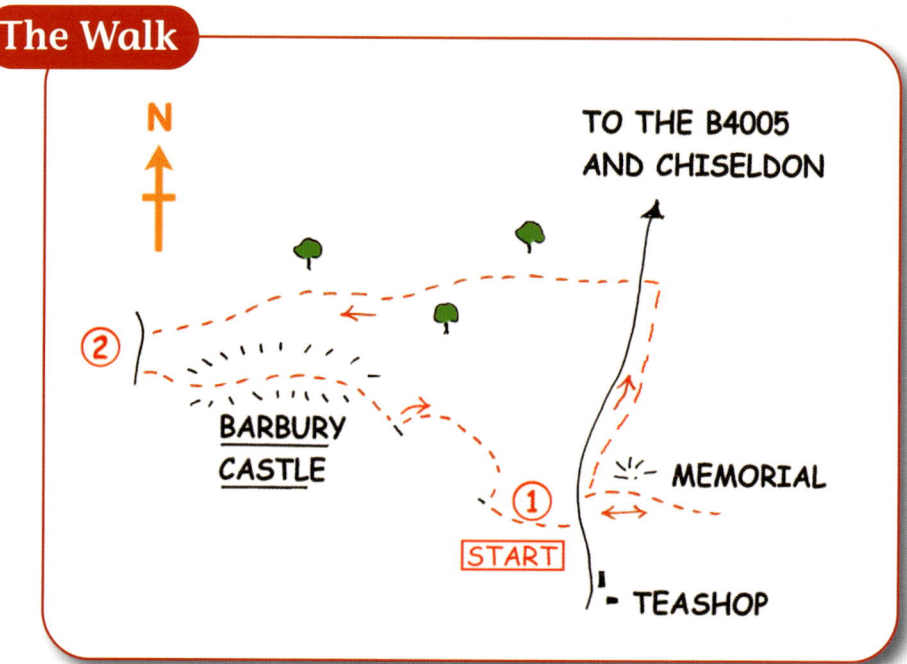

N

TO THE B4005 AND CHISELDON

②

BARBURY CASTLE

MEMORIAL

①

START

TEASHOP

Barbury Castle

1 Turn left out of the car park and follow the access road to the left downhill for 100 yards to a gate and stile on the right. Cross the stile and walk along to the Jefferies Memorial Stone. Retrace your steps to the road and turn right, dropping downhill for ¼ mile to a track on the left-hand side. Turn left and follow this track for ¾ mile to a lane.

2 Turn left and, in 50 yards, pass through a gate on the left and take the path uphill to the ramparts of Barbury Castle. Follow the right-hand ramparts around to a path at the eastern end of the hillfort. Turn right and continue on this path to a handgate. Beyond this gate, turn left down towards a line of trees. On reaching the trees, turn right and walk alongside the line of a

◆ Fun Things to See and Do ◆

 Hilltop sites – especially those blessed with a hillfort – are great fun for youngsters. The **ramparts and ditches** are ideal places to allow imaginations to run riot as children re-enact battles from centuries past. Hilltops are also wonderful places for **flying kites**, with breezes and winds providing the perfect conditions.

Hilltops with expansive outlooks have long inspired poets and writers. In the case of Barbury Castle, it was Alfred Williams. After toiling as a manual labourer in the railway workshops in Swindon, Williams would walk on the local hills and breathe in their unique atmosphere. **Take along a notebook** and, sitting alongside the monument to Williams on the hilltop, see if the family can come up with anything to rival 'Down in the Lowlands':

Down in the lowlands there grew a tree,
As fine a tree as you ever did see;
Tree was in the wood,
And the wood it was down in the lowlands low.

4

fence to reach a stile. Cross this stile, turn right and follow the hilltop back along to a handgate and the Barbury Castle car park.

The Jefferies Memorial Stone.

◆ Background Notes ◆

Barbury Castle is an Iron Age hillfort with two ramparts and accompanying ditches enclosing a site of some 12 acres. Evidence would suggest that the enclosure was occupied as a town, with aerial photography revealing huts and storage pits. This must have been a tremendously strong hillfort, with any prospective invaders facing strenuous hillside climbing before reaching the site breathless and unfit for battle. Just south of Barbury Castle, the OS map shows a battlefield site sandwiched between a wood and a country lane. The battle was Beranburh, fought in AD 556, when 'Cynric and Caewlin fought against the Britons' according to the Anglo Saxon Chronicle.

A sarsen stone monument along the way has been erected in memory of Wiltshire's greatest pastoral writers, **Richard Jefferies and Alfred Williams**. Jefferies, a one-time reporter on the *North Wiltshire Herald*, wrote many books that drew heavily on the people, places and natural history of his beloved downland. Williams, who was more of a poet, produced some quite inspirational work, including *Nature and Other Poems* and *Villages of the White Horse*. The monument records two inscriptions:

Alfred Williams 1877–1930
Still to find and still to follow
Joy in every hill and hollow
Company in solitude.

Richard Jefferies 1848–1887
It is eternity now.
I am in the midst of it.
It is about me in the sunshine.

5

Ford and the By Brook

Into the Valley

An inquisitive local.

S tep aside from the main road at Ford and you will find yourself in the tranquil and picturesque valley of the By Brook. This delightful tributary stream has its source above Castle Combe before flowing through Ford, Slaughterford and Box to its confluence with the Bristol Avon at Bathford. The valley can boast a range of different habitats – meadows and riverbanks, woodland and open hilltop – and provides the perfect setting for an appealing country walk.

Kiddiwalks in Wiltshire

Getting there *Ford lies 5 miles east of Cold Ashton on the A420 road to Chippenham. Park in a lay-by on the main road opposite the church.*

Length of walk 2¾ miles.
Time 2 hours.
Terrain Field paths and tracks.
Start/Parking The lay-by opposite the church in Ford (GR 841749).

Map OS Explorer 156 Chippenham & Bradford-on-Avon.
Refreshments The White Hart at Ford is an excellent inn, with a good number of picnic tables in its attractive gardens that border the By Brook.

1 Facing the church, follow the verge alongside the A420 to the right along to a left turn to Castle Combe. Beyond this left turn, continue following a verge

The Walk

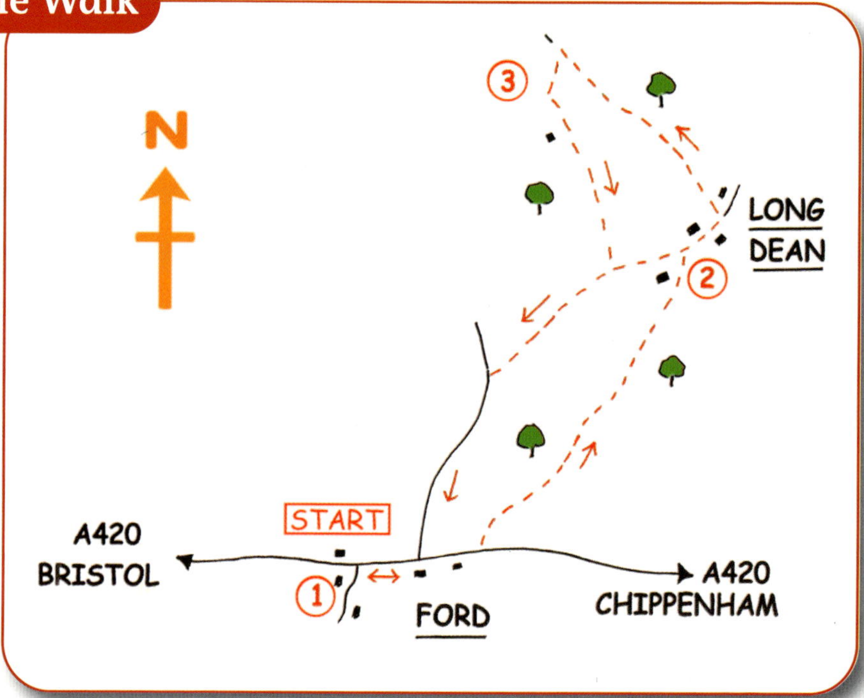

N

③

LONG DEAN

②

START

A420 BRISTOL

①

FORD

A420 CHIPPENHAM

Ford and the By Brook

alongside the A420 for 200 yards to a gate and footpath on the left. Walk across a field to a gap opposite before crossing a second field to a stile. Continue along a path through Fountain Wood before crossing a stile to enter a field. Cross this field – the path occasionally passing through bushes alongside the By Brook – to reach a bridge. Cross the By Brook before following the right edge of the next field to another footbridge. Re-cross the river and walk the length of the next field to a stile by a bridge before joining a track.

2 Turn right, and follow this track into the hamlet of Long Dean. At a junction in front of Rose Cottage – with a letterbox in the wall – turn left and take the track out of Long Dean uphill for 200 yards to a pair of gates on the hilltop. Continue following a woodland path across the hillside for 350 yards until an open field appears on the left-hand side of the track. At this point, turn sharp left on a footpath going steeply downhill into a field alongside the By Brook.

3 Follow the river downstream – with the river on the right – to a footbridge. Cross the By Brook to emerge by an isolated

◆ Fun Things to See and Do ◆

The By Brook is a clean and virtually unpolluted river, where **trout bask in the sparkling waters**. The river also attracts a wide range of wildfowl including kingfishers and herons, dippers and moorhens, whilst the surrounding meadows and woodland are home to such birds of prey as the buzzard and kestrel, as well as the occasional tawny and brown owl. It is worth taking a pair of binoculars along on this walk – plus a book of British birds – to see how many species you can spot. It is also worth bringing wellies, so that the children can enjoy **a paddle** on warm days at one or two points along the way where shallow water is easily accessible from the riverbank.

Roots galore.

cottage. Turn left and follow the river downstream for 500 yards to a stile and a track in Long Dean. Turn right, and follow this track uphill to a gateway on the hilltop. Continue along the track into an open field, before following the line of a fence across the hilltop to a stile in 100 yards. Cross this stile and walk across the hillside to a stile at the far end of the field. Join the Castle Combe to Ford road, turning left down to its junction with the A420 and then right back to the lay-by.

Ford and the By Brook

◆ Background Notes ◆

The **By Brook**, running from the Southern Cotswolds, is surely the most picturesque of the Avon's tributaries. Above Ford, it flows through a narrow, flat-bottomed valley with interlocking spurs of land on either side. The land along the brook is composed of a variety of flat grazing meadows and cultivated fields, with the banks having willows, alders and intermittent small scrubby bushes that provide cover for the abundant birdlife.

A **rich array of wildfowl** can be seen along the By Brook during each month of the year. Many common woodland species can be found along the valley, including nuthatches, treecreepers and green, great and lesser-spotted woodpeckers. Perhaps the main attractions are the dippers – in evidence wherever there is fast-flowing water – and the kingfishers, which burrow their nest holes in vertical riverside banks along the course of the brook.

Other than Ford, the only other settlement along the way is **Long Dean**. Pevsner recorded a 'pretty group of mill and 18th-century cottages in a combe', a succinct description of what is an almost prefect rural idyll. Accessible along a narrow cul de sac lane, Long Dean is surely as far from the proverbial madding crowd as it is possible to get in this neck of the woods. It was the river that originally created this remote settlement, with the faster sections of the By Brook being harnessed for their power during the heyday of the West of England woollen trade.

6

Brown's Folly Nature Reserve

Rocks, Quarries and Fossils

'Is anyone in there?'

T he Avon Valley between Bath and Bradford-on-Avon provides some of the finest walking in the region. The Avon flows through the valley bottom, bounded on both sides by wooded slopes rising to over 600 feet above sea-level, hillsides that were once quarried for their rich and colourful limestone. The Brown's Folly Reserve clings to one of these hillsides, with its tree cover masking many rock faces and boulders. From the occasional open clearing, spectacular views open up across the valley – extending beyond the Avon itself towards the Georgian terraces of Bath, properties constructed from the golden stone that lies underfoot. A walk sitting literally on the western border of the county that blends natural history with industrial history.

Brown's Folly Nature Reserve

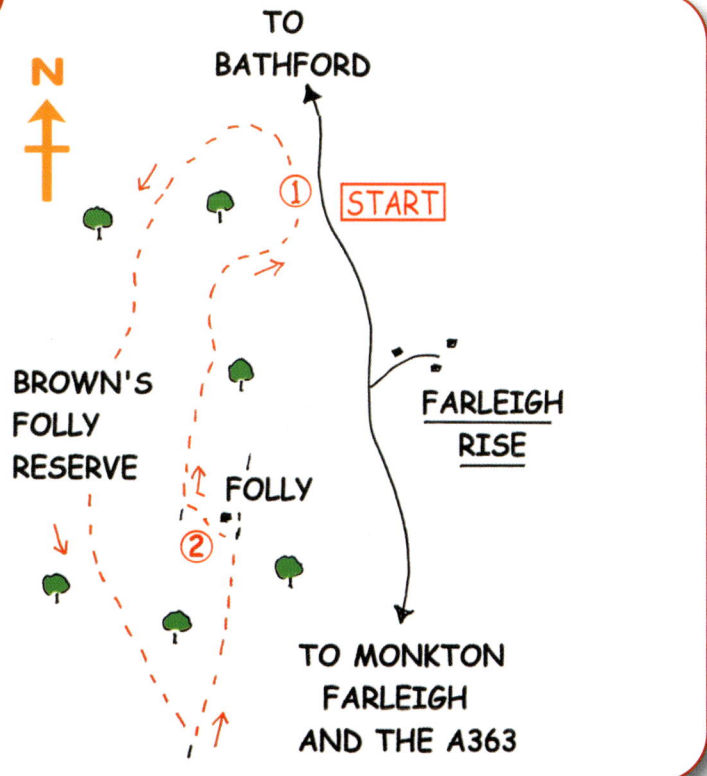
Getting there *The A363 runs between the A4 at Batheaston and Bradford-on-Avon. Drive 2 miles south of the A4 and turn left along a road signposted to Monkton Farleigh. At a junction in the village, turn left and follow a road to Farleigh Rise. In ½ mile, just as this lane begins to drop downhill, turn left into the woodland car park.*

Length of walk 1¾ miles.
Time 1½ hours.
Terrain Wooded slopes and open clearing above the Avon Valley, with the occasional steep slope along the way.
Start/Parking Brown's Folly Reserve free car park (GR 798663).
Map OS Explorer 155 Bristol & Bath.

The Walk

N

TO
BATHFORD

① START

BROWN'S
FOLLY
RESERVE

FARLEIGH
RISE

FOLLY

②

TO MONKTON
FARLEIGH
AND THE A363

Kiddiwalks in Wiltshire

6

Refreshments The King's Arms in Monkton Farleigh is an ancient inn with a reputation for being one of the most haunted pubs in the county. The open clearing on the walk above the Avon Valley makes a perfect spot for a picnic with views.

1 Pass through a gap in a fence at the lower end of the car park by a gate. Follow a woodland path for ½ mile before climbing uphill to a junction, ignoring various tracks that veer off to the left uphill along the way. At this junction, turn right and continue for another ¼ mile to a junction with another path on the hilltop, just below the boundary wall of the Brown's Folly Reserve. Turn left and

◆ Fun Things to See and Do ◆

Old quarries are both exciting and dangerous places. As you walk around the Brown's Folly Reserve, you will spot **rock faces and boulders** now overgrown with plants and shrubs. Some of these rocks are quite safe – and fun – to scramble on, others are loose and unstable. You might also spot the occasional cave or rock shelter. Most of these have been 'fenced off' to prevent the local bat population from being disturbed, but if you look carefully along the way, there are still one or two **open caves** to explore.

The stone in the reserve is limestone, which was formed millions of years ago when a shallow sea covered this part of the world. Small sea-creatures would fall to the bottom of this sea and, over a period of time, the pressure would cause their bodies and shells to solidify into rock. If the children look carefully at some broken pieces of limestone, they may well spot the **fossilised remains** of some ancient sea creature. On hot days, the exposed stone becomes a suntrap where **lizards and slow worms** may occasionally appear. These creatures are quite harmless, but are very delicate … so do avoid handling them.

Brown's Folly seen through the trees.

follow the path alongside this boundary wall for 600 yards to reach Brown's Folly.

2 Just by the folly, pass through a handgate on the left and follow a stepped path down the wooded hillside. At the bottom of the steps, follow the middle path on the right that climbs a bank onto an open clearing with fine views of the Avon Valley and Bath. Walk across to a gate on the far side of this hillside clearing, before following a woodland path that passes to the left of a cave. Continue along this path for 350 yards to some steps on the left before dropping down to the car park.

◆ Background Notes ◆

Stone mining took place for many years below what is now the Brown's Folly Nature Reserve. **Brown's Folly** itself was built in 1848 by a Mr Wade Brown who owned the local quarry. Local legend maintains that it was constructed during a time of economic depression by its benevolent owner to provide employment for the local working classes. An alternative perspective is that the folly – and its accompanying publicity – would provide a wonderful marketing opportunity for Wade Brown's stone! Yet another theory suggests that with Beckford's Tower to the north of Bath having dominated the city's skyline for some 15 years, it was a question of 'getting in on the act'. Architecturally, the folly has an Italian look to the top, but is otherwise rather plain.

The woodland and open spaces around the folly form a **nature reserve**, owned and managed by the Avon Wildlife Trust. To quote their website: 'The extensive remains of Bath stone quarries provide a rich variety of wildlife habitats. A delightful downland flora has covered the spoil heaps where wild thyme, harebell and nine species of orchid are found. The old mines offer a safe sanctuary for the threatened greater horseshoe bat, while damp cliff faces support a fascinating variety of ferns, fungi and spiders. Secondary woodland of ash with sycamore has grown up over the downland which once cloaked the hillside. Pockets of ancient woodland on the lower slopes are home to woodpeckers and unusual plants such as Bath asparagus.'

Lacock and the River Avon

A Town in a Time Warp

'Anyone for a sticky bun?' – the delightful bakery in Lacock.

This is a gentle walk alongside the River Avon in and around the picture postcard village of Lacock. The National Trust owns and manages the greater part of the village, and consequently there are few concessions to the 21st century. Along the way there is much to catch the eye, with the various attractions including Lacock Abbey, the Fox Talbot Museum, a historic tithe barn, riverbank wildlife and the village of Lacock itself. Described as 'easily the most remarkable and the most beautiful in Wiltshire', this is a village that attracts visitors from quite literally across the globe.

Kiddiwalks in Wiltshire

7

Getting there *Lacock lies just off the main A350 trunk road between Chippenham and Melksham. As you enter the village, follow the signs for the visitors' car park.*

Length of walk 2½ miles.
Time 2 hours.

Terrain A flat and easy walk. If there has been heavy rainfall you should be prepared for some mud on the paths alongside the River Avon.
Start/Parking The visitors' pay & display car park in Lacock, (free to NT members). (GR 918682).

◆ Fun Things to See and Do ◆

The medieval cloistered abbey, subsequently converted into a fine country house, is surrounded by beautiful gardens which are fun for children to explore. The abbey itself has featured in two Harry Potter films, which has ensured its celebrity status amongst the younger generation. The abbey's cloisters and side rooms were transformed into the classrooms of **Hogwarts School**, while the location was also used for Harry's discovery of the Mirror of Erised.

The River Avon between Lacock and Reybridge meanders across a clay vale that, in the days before flood relief schemes and sluice gates, would have been frequently under water. This is evident from the raised causeways at both Lacock and Reybridge. An **assortment of flora and fauna** have their habitat along this section of the river – it should not be difficult in the summer months to spot dragonflies, water lilies, teasels and moorhens along the course of the river, with timid rabbits feeding alongside in the riverside meadows. In Lacock, a ford through the Bide Brook – a tributary of the Avon – at point 2 of the walk provides the perfect spot for **pond dipping**. The Bide Brook is shallow, slow moving and easy to get at, making it a very safe spot for youngsters.

Lacock and the River Avon

The Walk

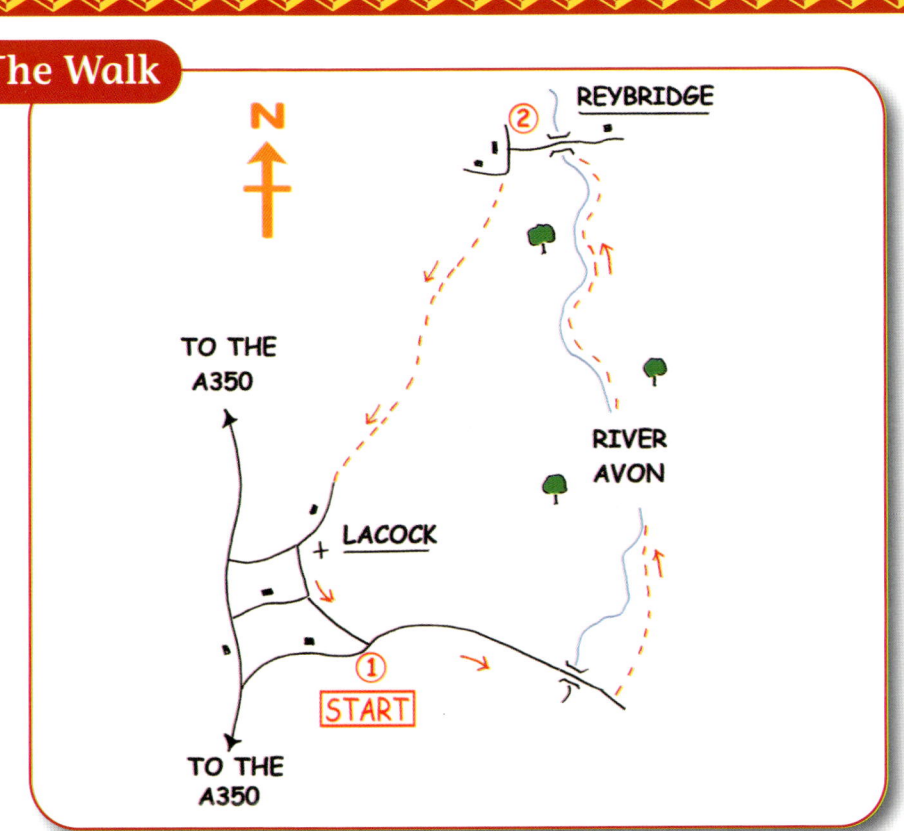

Map OS Explorer 156 Chippenham & Bradford-on-Avon.

Refreshments With three fine pubs and an equal number of teashops, there is no shortage of places to eat and drink in Lacock.

1 Leave the car park, turn right and follow the road as it bears right to head out of Lacock. Having crossed the River Avon in 350 yards, go over a stile on the left and follow a fieldpath across a large open field. Aim for the right-hand of two telegraph poles on the far side of the field, alongside which is a stile. In the following field, turn left and walk down to a gate, before crossing the next field to a gate and stile. Drop down to the banks of the Avon, and follow the river upstream across two fields to join the road in Reybridge.

2 Turn left, cross the Avon and, at a junction in front of a pair of thatched cottages, turn left. In 25 yards, where the road bears right, follow the tarmac path ahead between two cottages along to a handgate and open field. Follow the path across this field to a handgate by an aerial mast and join a lane. Turn left and follow the lane down to the church in Lacock, crossing a footbridge alongside a ford along the way. Turn right into Church Street, and then first left into East Street. At its junction with the High Street, turn left to return to the visitors' car park.

◆ Background Notes ◆

Lacock dates back to Saxon times – if not earlier. The village is based around four streets – Church Street, West and East Streets and the High Street – and still very much resembles a medieval town. Its attractive houses cover every century from the 13th to the 18th, with little more recent development to spoil the overall effect. The whole is admirably overseen and managed by the National Trust, with even the local telephone box being an unobtrusive shade of grey! William Fox Talbot, a gentleman scholar of considerable means and social standing, was a keen student of the arts and sciences. His experiments in the mid 1830s led him to discover the negative/positive photographic process, effectively making him the inventor of photography. The **Fox Talbot Museum** celebrates the life and work of a one-time resident of the adjoining abbey.

A riverbank walk across the Avon's floodplain brings the walk to the diminutive hamlet of **Reybridge**, whose delightful cottages and farmhouses are grouped around an ancient bridge that spans the river. From here, it is but a short walk across the fields back into Lacock, following a path whose slight elevation brings surprisingly good views. Immediately at hand is the river, beyond which – and several hundred feet higher – lie the Naish and Bowden Hills, rising to nearly 600 feet above sea-level. The more gentle slopes of this higher land are given over to arable farming, with woodland emerging on the higher slopes.

Cherhill

White Horse Country

Cherhill's White Horse, with the Lansdowne Monument to the right.

A n initial climb brings the walk onto Cherhill Down, where the ramparts of Oldbury Castle stand at some 800 feet above sea-level. Below this ancient hillfort lies the Cherhill White Horse, whilst alongside stands the imposing Landsdowne Monument, a vast 125 ft tall obelisk. All around lie vast tracts of unimproved chalk downland whose unique flora attracts a rich array of butterflies in summer. There are also fine views from this lofty hilltop, extending across vast tracts of the North Wiltshire countryside.

8

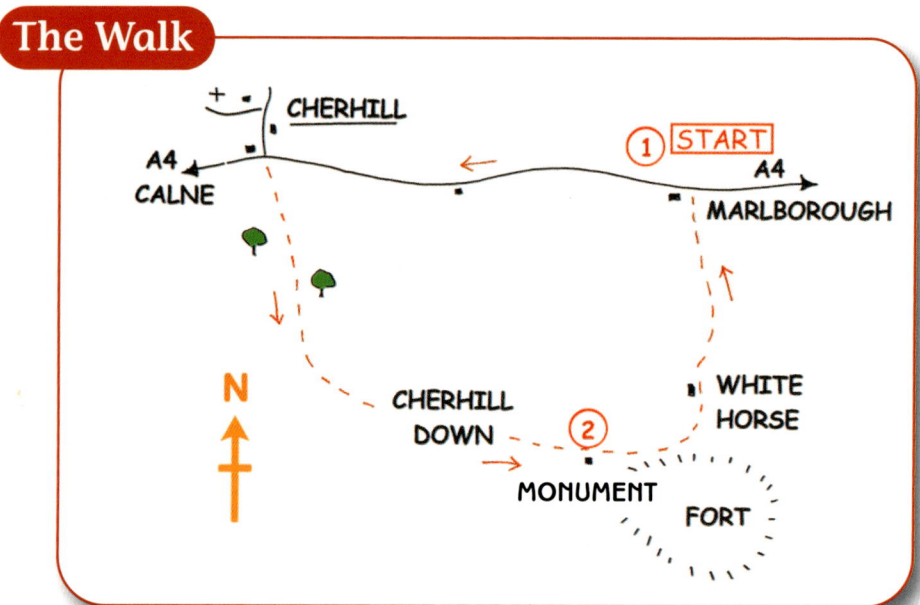

Getting there *Cherhill lies on the A4 between Calne and Beckhampton. Approaching from the west, drive through the village and, 400 yards beyond the last property on the left – and at the top of a gentle climb – park in a lay-by on the right just below a property.*

Length of walk 2 miles.
Time 2 hours.
Terrain A stiff climb of some 450 ft onto Cherhill Down, followed by an equally steep descent at journey's end but nothing too daunting.

Start/Parking A lay-by on the A4 at Cherhill, 3 miles east of Calne (GR 045702).
Map OS Explorer 157 Marlborough & Savernake Forest.
Refreshments On the A4 in Cherhill, heading towards Calne, you will find the Divine Café, which offers home cooked, healthy food and freshly baked cakes. Alternatively, on a fine summer's day, the hilltop with its expansive outlook and traditional chalk grassland is the perfect place for a picnic.

1 Cross the A4 to a pavement opposite, turn left and walk

The Walk

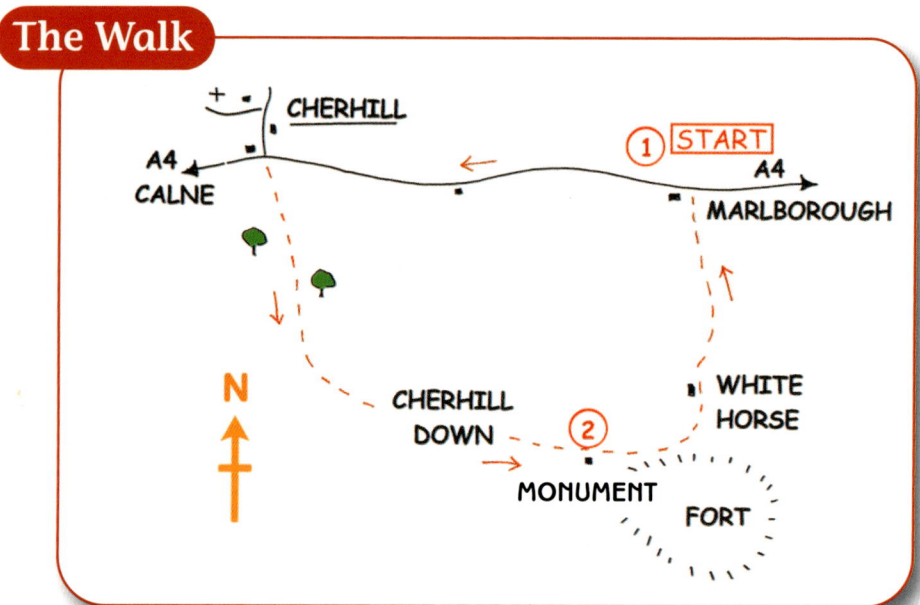

◆ Fun Things to See and Do ◆

Most of the grassland on Cherhill Down is unimproved, so has never been ploughed or treated with artificial fertilisers. This means that a **wide diversity of wild flowers** remains. The changing seasons bring a rich array of flora including cowslips and violets in the spring, orchids in the summer, and devil's bit and small scabious in the autumn. The hilltop is also important for **butterflies**, and on a warm summer day the ground is alive with species such as common blue, marbled white, and a particular rarity is the nationally scarce Duke of Burgundy. Be sure to bring a spotter's guide on this particular walk to see how many species your youngsters can identify.

The hilltop site also provides all sorts of opportunities for fun and relaxation. The ramparts of the hillfort, for example, will provide the perfect location for **re-enacting battles from centuries past**. The exposed hilltop is also a perfect spot for **kite flying**. If your visit to Cherhill coincides with a windy day, then be sure to pack a kite into that rucksack.

downhill back towards Cherhill. On the edge of the village, opposite Park Lane on the right, cross the main road and follow an enclosed track opposite that heads uphill towards Cherhill Down. In 400 yards, cross a stile at the top of the bank on the left and enter an open field. Turn right, and follow the line of a fence on the right

The monument in close-up.

uphill to the top corner of the field. In the corner of the field, turn left and follow a grassy path up to the Lansdowne Monument.

2 Pass to the left of this obelisk, and continue following a path that runs across the edge of the hilltop, with the ramparts of Oldbury Castle on the right. In 200 yards, keep on the path as it bears left to pass above the Cherhill White Horse. Continue following the well-worn path as it drops downhill to reach a clearly visible track. Follow this track to the right across a cattle grid and along a tree-lined course back to the A4. Turn left and walk past a property called Poachers Croft, back to the lay-by.

◆ Background Notes ◆

Oldbury Hillfort, dating back to the Iron Age, covers a site of some 20 acres. The site lies protected by a double bank and ditch, with a clear inturned entrance being visible on its eastern end.

The fort overlooks the **Cherhill White Horse**, cut in 1780 by a Doctor Christopher Alsop of nearby Calne. Nicknamed the 'mad doctor' because of his efforts in constructing this hill figure, his inspiration was probably the recently re-cut horse at Westbury. Tradition has it that the doctor stood one mile from the hillside with some sort of megaphone, shouting instructions to his men on the site who would mark out the figure's outline using white flags. The top turf could then be removed, and the cavity filled with chalk to form the figure. Rumour has it that when the local populace were opposing the construction of the Great Western Railway, many local coaching jobs depending upon the Great West Road that passes through Cherhill, Brunel – the GWR's engineer – was tempted to convert the white horse into a locomotive-shape under cover of darkness!

The **Landsdowne Monument** of 1845, erected by the 3rd Marquess of Lansdowne on the highest point along the Great West Road between London and Bath, commemorates his ancestor, the 17th-century economist Sir William Petty.

Avebury

Magical Stones

The fascinating stones in The Avenue.

A round the village of Avebury lies one of the most ancient and mysterious landscapes in Britain. The imprints of ancient civilisation are everywhere – a vast stone circle, a long barrow, round barrows, ancient tracks and unexplained mounds. Such is the importance of the area that UNESCO has granted it World Heritage status, which is only conferred on sites of outstanding cultural or natural importance to the common heritage of humanity. The mysterious element continues to this day, with crop circles appearing each summer in the arable fields surrounding the village. This is truly a walk into the pages of ancient history, with interest and intrigue at every turn.

Kiddiwalks in Wiltshire

9

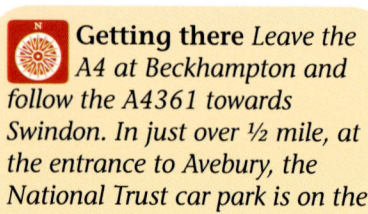

Getting there *Leave the A4 at Beckhampton and follow the A4361 towards Swindon. In just over ½ mile, at the entrance to Avebury, the National Trust car park is on the left-hand side of the main road.*

Length of walk 3 miles.
Time 2 hours.
Terrain A flat landscape with just one gentle climb to visit the West Kennet Long Barrow.
Start/Parking The National Trust car park (fee payable) alongside the A4361 in Avebury (GR 100697).

The Walk

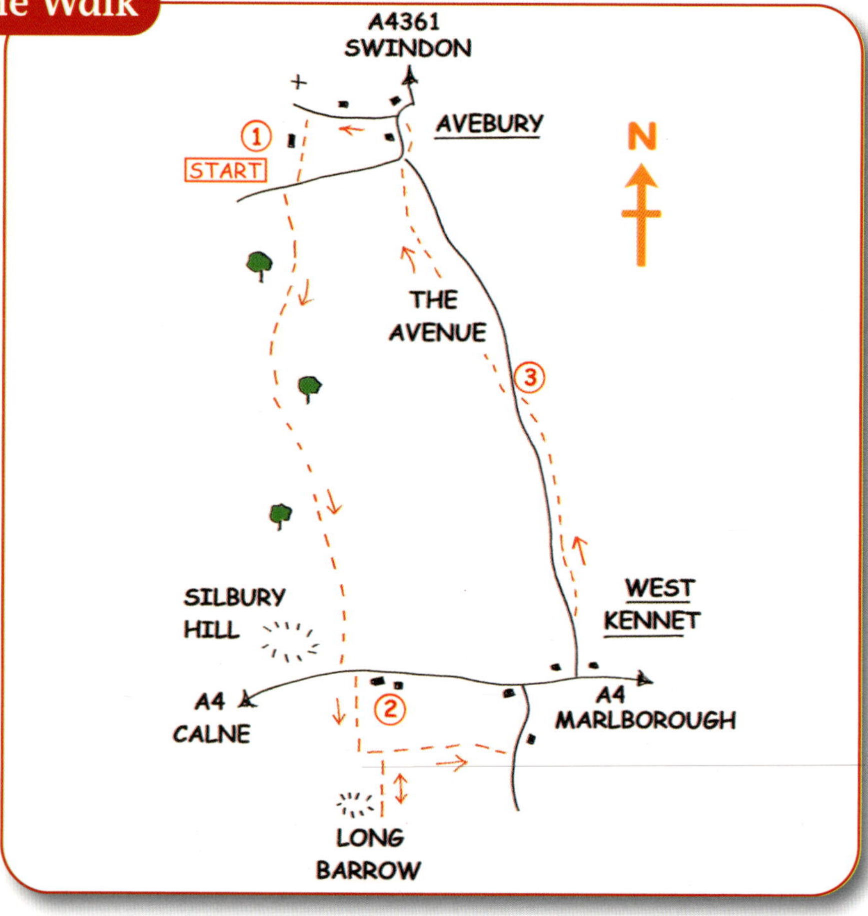

A4361
SWINDON

① START

AVEBURY

N

THE AVENUE

③

SILBURY HILL

WEST KENNET

A4 CALNE

②

A4 MARLBOROUGH

LONG BARROW

Avebury

Map OS Explorer 157 Marlborough & Savernake Forest. **Refreshments** The Red Lion at Avebury is a family-friendly pub with a number of picnic tables, as well as high chairs in its eating areas. The Circle Restaurant in the village is a haven for vegetarians, and enjoys a fine location in the heart of the stone circle.

◆ Fun Things to See and Do ◆

The River Kennet borders the footpath during the early part of the walk. A clear chalk stream where watercress abounds, it has its source near Avebury before flowing on through Marlborough and Newbury to join the Thames at Reading.

Long barrows were constructed in centuries past as burial places for ancient people. When it was excavated in the 1950s, the remains of between 40 and 50 people were discovered in West Kennet Long Barrow – some of which were children. The oldest of the remains were dated back to 2570 BC and the barrow itself was in use for around a thousand years. This is one of the few **long barrows** that can be explored internally, so be sure to bring a torch on this particular walk to explore the dark and scary heart of this burial site.

The **embankment that surrounds the ancient stone circle** at Avebury will provide the perfect spot for expending energy at journey's end. Children will enjoy marching along the top of this vast earthwork, as well as running up and down its steep sides. The stones that make up the circle are themselves strange and mysterious objects. Children will have great fun trying to **identify which of the stones resemble faces** with features such as noses and eyes clearly identifiable.

Behind the stones lies the entrance to the Long Barrow.

1 Walk out of the car park onto the A4361 and turn right. In 20 yards, cross to a handgate opposite and walk through a small paddock to another handgate and a path alongside the River Kennet. Follow this path for ¼ mile to a handgate and a bridge over the river. Do not cross the river – instead continue following the riverside path for 40 yards before crossing a stile on the left. Turn right to another stile and continue following the riverside path along to a handgate. Walk along the right edge of a field down to a gate and the A4. Silbury Hill can be seen in the distance. Cross the main road with care, turn left and, in a few paces, pass through a handgate on the right to follow a path to the West Kennet Long Barrow. Follow the path ahead to a gate just beyond the River Kennet. Keep on the path as it bears left to reach a solitary tree on the left in 40 yards. At this point, *a detour to the right* up the hill will bring you to the long barrow.

2 *For the main walk*, keep ahead across the left edge of the field to a gate and stile in the corner. Continue along a track to a lane and turn left. Cross the River Kennet and walk up to the A4. Turn right and walk along the verge for 100 yards, then turn left by West Kennet Farm along

an unmarked road – technically the B4003 to Avebury. Follow the B4003 towards Avebury for 150 yards, cross a stile on the right and turn left to follow a field path running alongside the road. Almost in the corner of the field, cross a stile on the left and cross the B4003 to a stile opposite.

3 Enter a field and follow its right-hand boundary to a handgate in the corner of the field. Enter an enclosure containing a series of stones known as 'The Avenue'. Walk the whole length of this enclosure through to Avebury, passing through a handgate at the end of the enclosure. Cross a road to a gate opposite, turn left and walk through a beech clump. Continue along the length of a field containing part of Avebury's stone circle, towards the Red Lion pub. At the end of the field, pass through a handgate and cross the busy A4361 to reach the Red Lion. Turn left and, in a few paces, where the main road bears left, keep ahead, walking down through Avebury's High Street. In 100 yards, opposite a rank of brick cottages on the right, turn left along an enclosed path signposted to the National Trust car park. Follow this path back to the car park.

◆ Background Notes ◆

That this is important countryside for the archaeologist is clear from the fact that at one time three of the monuments on this walk received a mention in the *Guinness Book of Records*. The **earthworks and stone circle at Avebury** are described as 'Britain's largest megalithic prehistoric monument', **Silbury Hill** is renowned for being the 'largest artificial mound in Europe' and the **West Kennet Long Barrow** is 'England's longest barrow containing a megalithic chamber'. Learned academics have written lengthy tomes on these strange and mysterious landmarks, speculating as to their origin and function. It is a body of literature that I feel quite incapable of adding to. Suffice to say that at each site there is an informative plaque from which the interested observer can learn more, whilst at Avebury itself a selection of excellent literature can be purchased.

Roundway Down

A Bloody Battle of the Civil War

Striding out to Oliver's Castle.

T he views from the ramparts of Oliver's Castle may provide a peaceful outlook today … but it was not always that way. Back in 1643, this was the scene of one of the bloodiest battles in the English Civil War. Located where the Wessex Downs meet the clay vale of the Bristol Avon, this is a short and very easy walk that will be within the capabilities of most children – even young toddlers, given time! The views in all directions are truly impressive – especially looking west from the hilltop – whilst the chalk downland is home to a rich and varied range of flowers and insects, birds and animals. A walk through history – both of the natural and political varieties.

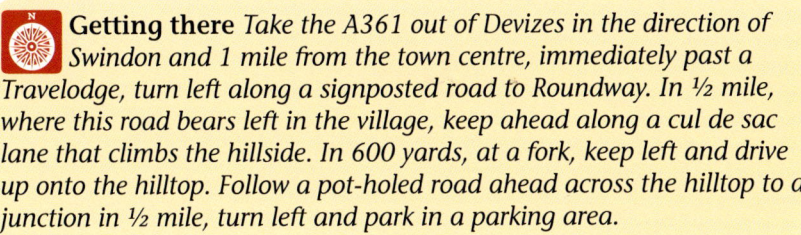

Getting there *Take the A361 out of Devizes in the direction of Swindon and 1 mile from the town centre, immediately past a Travelodge, turn left along a signposted road to Roundway. In ½ mile, where this road bears left in the village, keep ahead along a cul de sac lane that climbs the hillside. In 600 yards, at a fork, keep left and drive up onto the hilltop. Follow a pot-holed road ahead across the hilltop to a junction in ½ mile, turn left and park in a parking area.*

Length of walk 1½ miles.
Time 1½ hours.
Terrain A short and flat hilltop walk.

Start/Parking The free car park adjoining Oliver's Castle on Roundway Down (GR 005648).

The Walk

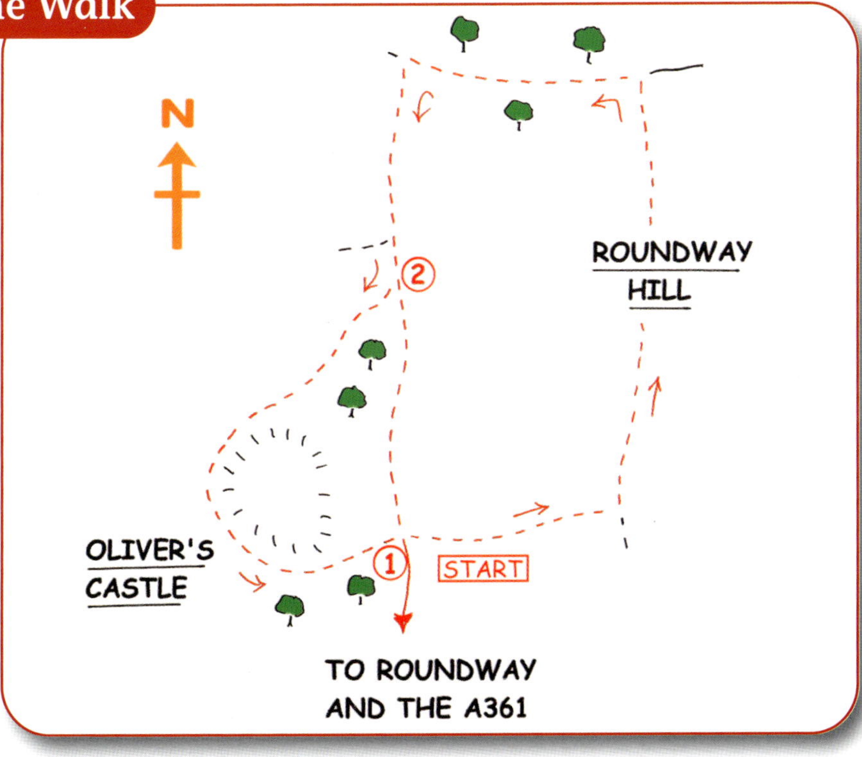

N

ROUNDWAY HILL

②

OLIVER'S CASTLE

① START

TO ROUNDWAY AND THE A361

Kiddiwalks in Wiltshire

Map OS Explorer 157 Marlborough & Savernake Forest. **Refreshments** There are no refreshment facilities on the walk, although Oliver's Castle with its fine outlook would make the perfect spot for a picnic. Back on the A361 in Devizes adjoining the Travelodge is a Subway restaurant selling the usual range of filled rolls, salads and wraps.

1 Walk back out of the parking area and follow a track out onto Roundway Hill, ignoring the pot-holed road on the right that heads back to Devizes. In 200 yards, turn left to take a prominent track beyond a metal barrier across the open hilltop for ¼ mile to a junction. Turn left and walk along a track for 350 yards to a track on the left-hand side. Turn left at this point, and follow a track across the hilltop for 350 yards to the second footpath on the right, ignoring the first path – the Mid Wilts Way.

◆ Fun Things to See and Do ◆

Hilltops are always good places for fun and relaxation and Roundway Down is no exception. As well as **kite flying** and **running amok on the ramparts of Oliver's Castle**, there is the opportunity to **slide down the hillsides** around the hillfort site. Many youngsters come armed with plastic fertiliser bags that slide with consummate ease down the grassy slopes below Oliver's Castle. The hilltop, with its vast outlook, is also quite the **perfect spot for a picnic** on a fine summer's day.

The unimproved chalk grassland around Oliver's Castle is home to a **rich variety of birds and insects, animals and flowers**. It should prove fairly straightforward, for example, to spot orchids and crows, beech trees and grazing sheep. **A fun challenge** is to list the 26 letters of the alphabet and to see if the children can find something to fit as many of these letters as possible. To get started, the 'B' could stand for buttercup and the 'L' for ladybird. A score of over 20 would be excellent, whilst anything over 15 is very good. Find something to fit every one of the 26 letters and it would be a miracle!

2 Pass through a handgate on the right and ahead there are two options. Do not follow the right-hand path that drops downhill through the escarpment – instead keep ahead, following a fence on the left along to a handgate. Beyond this gate, keep on the path as it bears left along the edge of the escarpment to reach the beech trees by Oliver's Castle. Continue following the edge of the hilltop, passing to the right of the beech trees, to reach the south-western corner of the hillfort. Keep on the path – it bears left – and follow the path along the edge of a hilltop overlooking the woodland of Roundway Hill Covert for 300 yards to a gate and track. Turn right to return to the car park.

What has she spotted in the grass?

Kiddiwalks in Wiltshire

◆ Background Notes ◆

The open downland that is crossed during the early part of this walk is today just peaceful countryside with extensive views all around. Had you been walking here in 1643, however, you may well have been diving for cover. This is **Roundway Down**, scene all those years ago of a battle during the English Civil War. It was here that Sir William Waller and his Parliamentary troops were attacked by Royalist forces. Sir William fled the site, endowing it with the name 'Runaway Hill'. This was later to become Roundway Hill as it is known today. An information board on the site records precise details of the battle, including such facts and figures as the 600 Parliamentary casualties.

Flower-rich grasslands have declined dramatically due to changes in agriculture, but Wiltshire is fortunate insofar as it contains over half of Britain's remaining **unimproved chalk grassland**. The chalk soil supports a unique collection of flowers in season, ranging from the spotted orchid and the field scabious to the harebell and the chalk milkwort. Attracted by all of the colourful plants and flowers in summer is an array of butterflies. The meadow brown, the peacock, the red admiral and the large white are especially common. Insects, too, are here in abundance – snails, aphids, slugs, ladybirds, bees and wasps. These in turn attract a varied number of birds, with the local arable crops providing a useful supplement to their diet. Finches, skylarks, pigeons, crows and kestrels are common hereabouts. This is a whole community of living creatures, an ecosystem as the scientists call it, with total interdependence between the various species.

Oliver's Castle is a univallate (one circuit of defences) promontory fort on a spur between Beacon Hill and Roundway Hill. Roughly triangular in shape with an entrance at the east, it encloses a site of some 3 acres. There are a pair of Bronze Age round barrows on the site, which command exceptional views that encompass the Avon Vale, Salisbury Plain and the more distant Cotswold Hills. Not only did the steep hillsides all around make this an uncomplicated site to defend, the extensive outlook would have made it easy to spot an enemy on the move some time before they approached this ancient hillfort.

Savernake Forest

If You Go Down to the Woods Today ...

Springtime in the forest.

The Woodland Trust make it very clear on their website as to why woodland matters. 'Woods are essential to life. They have a myriad of different benefits for both wildlife and people. They stabilise the soil, generate oxygen, store carbon, play host to a spectacular variety of wildlife provide us with raw materials and shelter, inspire our imaginations and our creativity. The almost magical, mystical quality of woods makes them a great place for relaxation and recreation. A walk in the woods can give anyone a feeling of peace and tranquillity. Most of us have fond childhood memories of playing on or around trees. A world without trees and woods would be barren and bare.' With all of this in mind, a woodland stroll in arguably one of southern Britain's greatest forests represents a rare treat.

11

Getting there *Turn south-west off the A346 just over 3 miles south of Marlborough, along an unclassified road signposted to Wootton Rivers and Brimslade. In 75 yards, turn left and park on the access road to a former picnic site.*

Length of walk 2½ miles.
Time 2 hours.
Terrain Flat and level woodland paths with no hills or inclines along the way.
Start/Parking The entrance to a former picnic site alongside the A346 south of Marlborough (GR 216647).
Map OS Explorer 157 Marlborough & Savernake.

The Walk

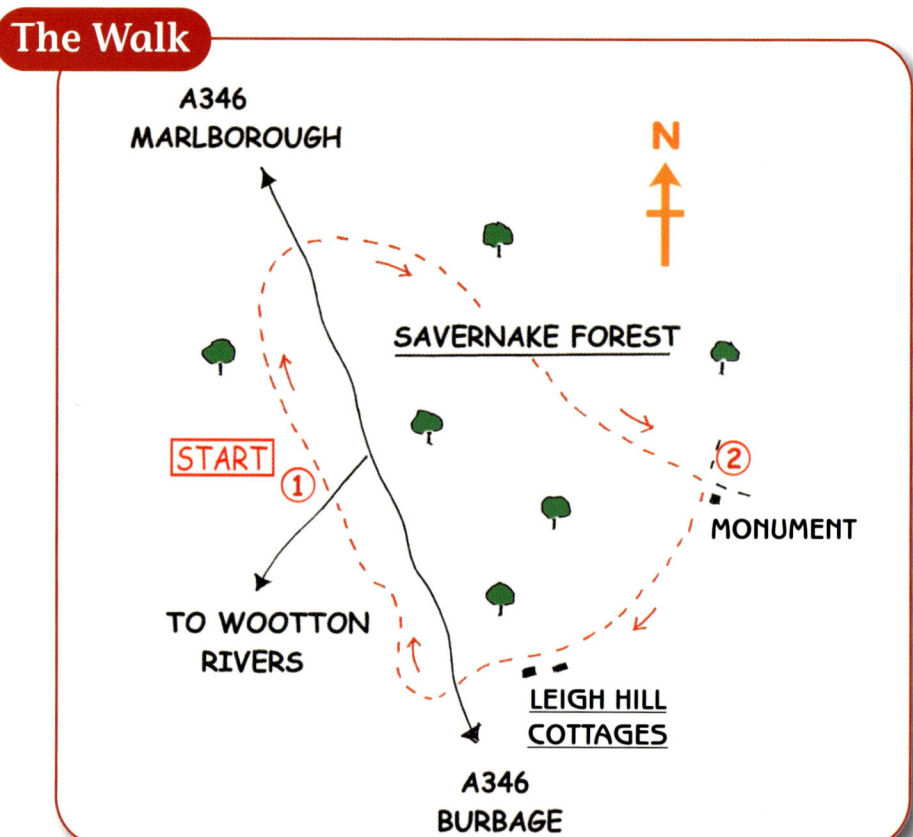

A346
MARLBOROUGH

N

SAVERNAKE FOREST

START ①

② MONUMENT

TO WOOTTON RIVERS

LEIGH HILL COTTAGES

A346 BURBAGE

Refreshments There are no pubs, cafés or tearooms along the way. Why not take a picnic? Or, at journey's end, you could head back to Marlborough where the Polly Tea Rooms, established in 1932, has become known as one of the best privately-owned tearooms in England.

1 Return to the road and follow the woodland path opposite beyond a wooden barrier. Continue on the woodland path for 600 yards to a point where it bears right down to the

The 100 ft tall Ailesbury Monument.

◆ Fun Things to See and Do ◆

Woodlands are magical places with their **secretive glades and abundant flora and fauna** … and Savernake Forest is no exception. **Deer** are frequent visitors but they are extremely timid creatures so you might have to sit quietly and still for some time before they will appear! Spring is an excellent time to come down to the woods, with so many **wild flowers** carpeting the ground. Wood anemone and celandine, primroses and bluebells are the most common species to look out for. Bring a wildlife guidebook with you and see how many different wild flowers you can recognize. Although, remember you must never pick wild flowers!

main A346. Cross with care and follow the woodland path opposite – again beyond a barrier – for just under 1 mile until it reaches the Ailesbury Monument.

2 Follow the track to the right by the monument – signposted as a private drive giving access to Leigh Hill Cottages – for ½ mile through to the A346. Cross the main road and follow a woodland path opposite – the path shortly bears right – through the woodland and down to the access road where your vehicle is parked.

◆ Background Notes ◆

Once an extensive medieval royal forest, **Savernake** still retains many aspects of its former glory, with relics of the mid-18th-century woodland, together with areas of scattered scrub and grassy glades. Massive sessile oaks, some of the largest sweet chestnuts in the country and beeches are the main forest trees. It is the open nature of much of the forest that makes it so good for birds and insects, particularly beetles and moths. Mosses, lichens and fungi also abound.

Although such **unusual birds** as the roller – a bright-blue visitor from the Continent – have been recorded in the forest, it is the more common scrub and woodland species such as nightingales, turtle doves, tree pipits, woodpeckers, nuthatches, tree-creepers, six species of tit and several warblers for which the forest is best known. With a bit of good fortune, wood warblers and redstarts may also be seen.

The **Ailesbury Monument** was erected in 1781 by Thomas Bruce, Earl of Ailesbury, as a monument to his uncle and benefactor Charles Earl of Ailesbury and Elgin. The inscription at the base of the column also pays homage to George III and to God.

Wilton and the Kennet & Avon Canal

A Peaceful Towpath and a Roman Road

The pumping station seen from the canal.

All canals have their summit levels and, in the case of the Kennet & Avon Canal, it is to be found at Crofton in the heart of Wiltshire. These high points often run dry as water is drained off to lower parts of the waterway. To prevent the K&A running dry, a reservoir – Wilton Water – was constructed at the summit level. Alongside stands Crofton Pumping Station, whose job was to raise water from this reservoir into the canal. Away from the canal and its industrial heritage, there are fine views across the local landscape from an ancient Roman road that runs across the hilltop between Wilton and Crofton. This is the archetypal 'low on miles but high on interest' walk.

12

Getting there *Turn off the A338 at East Grafton, east of Burbage, onto an unclassified road signposted to Wilton. As you drive into Wilton, park on the roadside by a pond on the right.*

Length of walk 1¾ miles.
Time 1½ hours.
Terrain A generally flat and easy walk, with just one short climb on

the Roman road between Wilton and Crofton.
Start/Parking The roadside by the village pond in Wilton (GR 267617).
Map OS Explorer 157 Marlborough & Savernake Forest.
Refreshments The Swan Inn at Wilton offers excellent food and drinks. Another alternative is the

The Walk

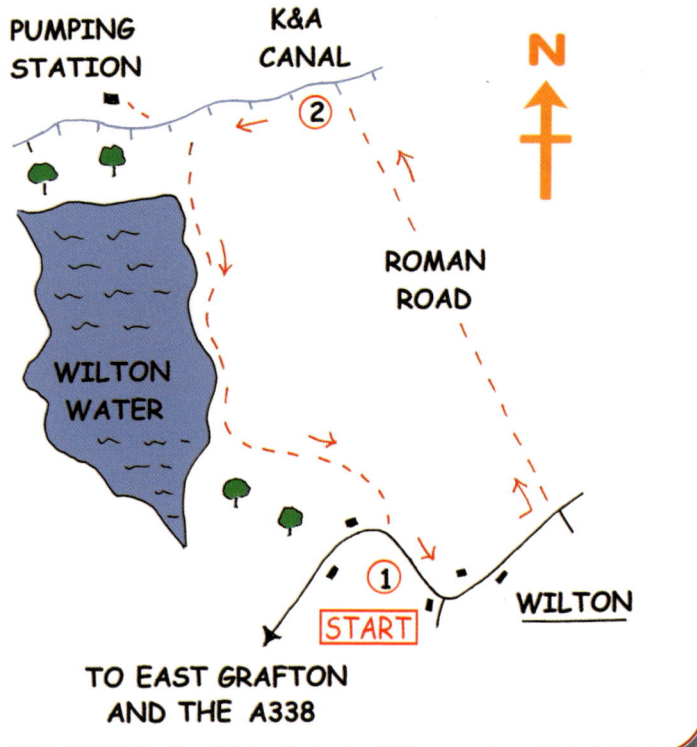

Wilton and the Kennet & Avon Canal

Engineman's Rest Café at Crofton Pumping Station, which offers freshly prepared local food in the summer months.

1 Continue following the road – with the pond on the right – along to the Swan Inn. Keep on the main road – it bears left – in the direction signposted to Great Bedwyn. In 250 yards, at a junction, follow the track on the left signposted to Crofton Beam Engines. Follow this track – a former Roman road – for ½ mile over a hilltop and down to the Kennet & Avon Canal.

2 Follow the towpath to the left for 200 yards and, immediately before a lock and Crofton Pumping Station, turn left onto a path that borders Wilton Water. (*To visit the pumping station,*

◆ Fun Things to See and Do ◆

Crofton Pumping Station contains a pair of working steam engines that pump water from the nearby Wilton Water into the Kennet & Avon Canal. During the summer months, the visiting public have access to all parts of the station, whether in steam or not and, when in steam, can experience close up the smell and sounds of these wonderful relics of our past in operation. Plan your walk for a day when the steam engines are working and you will be in for a real treat. Details of steam days can be found on the station's website: www.croftonbeamengines.org

Wilton Water is an excellent location for **bird watching**. It is a good site for breeding little grebe, Canada goose, mallard and tufted duck, with small numbers of teal, widgeon, gadwall and pochard also found in winter. Water tails are regular while more occasional visitors have included Slavonian grebe, red-breasted merganser and osprey. The odd common sandpiper or black tern sometimes stops briefly on migration. If all of these names mean nothing, be sure to take a bird identification book on this walk, together with a pair of binoculars … and maybe some bread to feed the ducks!

continue along the towpath and cross the canal using a 'footbridge' on the first set of lock gates.) Follow the path alongside the lake for ½ mile, crossing two fields. On the far side of the second field, bear right out of the field onto the lane alongside the pond in Wilton.

Narrowboats moored up on

◆ Background Notes ◆

The **Roman road** near Wilton is thought to be a section of the routeway that linked Cunetio (Mildenhall, near Marlborough) with Venta Belgarum (Winchester). Fortunately it has escaped the Highways Department and its tarmacadam, and still retains an authentic feel as a consequence. Fine views open up as the road crosses the crest of the hill, although Wilton Water is disappointingly out of sight in the valley below. Also out of eyeshot is the spire of Salisbury Cathedral, although local rumour has suggested that the 404-ft pinnacle can be seen from the hilltop!

At the summit level of any waterway, a reliable water supply is an absolute necessity. Literally hundreds of thousands of gallons of the precious liquid will be flowing through the locks in both directions. The K&A's supply comes from **Wilton Water**, an artificial lake, where steam engines were originally used to raise the water to the summit level. These engines were a pair of Cornish beam engines, an 1812 Boulton and Watt, together with an 1845 Harvey's of Hayle. Both have been carefully restored and returned to full working order and are believed to be the oldest operational steam engines in the world. Wilton Water is an 8-acre reservoir that was formed by damming a spring-fed stream that trickles down the valley from nearby Wilton. Water is lifted a height of 40 ft from Wilton Water to the canal's summit by way of Crofton Leat, a small channel that runs westwards for almost a mile from the pumping station to Crofton Top Lock.

Pewsey Downs and the Wansdyke

On a Clear Day, You Can See Forever

The clear path over the downs.

This walk lies entirely above the 700 ft contour line, as it crosses perhaps the finest downland within the North Wessex region. The views are vast, and the greater part of the landscape unspoiled by modern farming techniques due to its National Nature Reserve status. The going is generally straightforward, with just one steep ascent onto Adam's Grave, an ancient long barrow. When combined with the Wansdyke – a spectacular linear fortification – as well as one of the county's noted white horses, this is a circuit with historical intrigue at every turn. Be sure to pick a dry, clear day for this route, when the fine views can be fully appreciated.

Kiddiwalks in Wiltshire

13

Getting there *Follow the main road through the Vale of Pewsey between Devizes and Pewsey to a staggered crossroads in Alton Barnes. Take the road signposted to Marlborough uphill onto the downs. Park in the hilltop parking area alongside the road in 1 mile.*

Length of walk 2¾ miles.
Time 2 hours.
Terrain Grassy paths and woodland tracks.
Start/Parking Pewsey Downs Nature Reserve free car park (GR 116637).
Map OS Explorer 157 Marlborough & Savernake Forest.
Refreshments There are no refreshment facilities on the walk,

◆ Fun Things to See and Do ◆

Archaeology is the study of the past through material remains. High on these hilltops lies the **Wansdyke**, a fortification that has been described as southern Britain's version of Hadrian's Wall. This ancient landmark dates all the way back to the Dark Ages. As you walk, imagine what life was like when the bank was built. Would you be able to spot your enemies coming? This is the perfect place to **engage in a spot of role play**, emulating the Britons trying to defend their land from an invasion by pagan Saxons.

The Pewsey Downs National Nature Reserve is a haven for **rare wild flowers and unusual butterflies** in summer. A good spotter's guide is something of a must on this walk, but beware of grown adults on their hands-and-knees muttering strange expressions such as 'Orchis maculata' and 'Polygala vulgaris'.

The steep chalk escarpments around the Vale of Pewsey also provide opportunities to **watch the more energetic activities of hang gliding and paragliding**. Children always enjoy seeing these light and unmotorised foot-launchable aircraft floating effortless in the skies above the clay vale.

The Walk

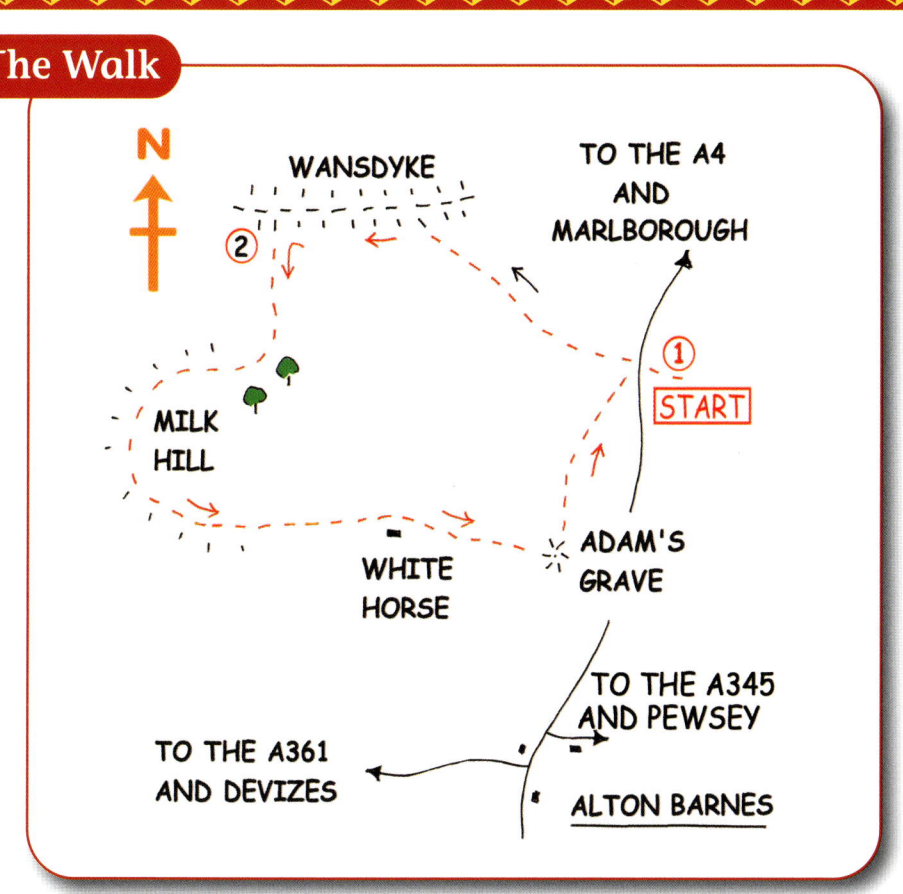

but the open downs present many opportunities for a picnic. Alternatively, head south from the hilltops to Honeystreet, just beyond Alton Barnes, and you will find the excellent Barge Inn with its idyllic location alongside the Kennet & Avon Canal.

1 Leave the car park, cross the road and pass through a gateway opposite. Follow a fieldpath ahead uphill – with a fence on the left – across two fields. Beyond the second field, continue along a track to reach the Wansdyke. Pass through a gate on the left immediately past the Wansdyke and climb up onto this linear fortification. Follow the line of the Wansdyke in a westerly direction for 400 yards to a stile and track. Cross this track and pass through a handgate opposite alongside a Pewsey Downs National Nature Reserve information board.

2 Follow the left edge of the field ahead to a handgate, before following the left edge of a second field – with a steep hillside on the right – through to another gate. Head across a third field to a further gate, this one to the right of a wooded enclosure. Beyond this gate, continue following the line of the fence on the left across the hilltop. Where this fence forms a corner, turn left and follow a path across the hillside high above the Vale of Pewsey. Beyond a handgate, continue along the path as it passes above the Alton Barnes White Horse. Keep on the path as it goes through an area of gorse bushes before continuing onto the prominent summit of Walkers Hill, the site of Adam's Grave. With your back to the Vale of Pewsey, the car park is clearly visible some 350 yards distant. Walk back to the car park, crossing stiles in fences along the way.

'We're heading this way!'

Background Notes ◆

The origin and purpose of the **Wansdyke**, a two-part bank and ditch created in the Dark Ages, are obscure. A defensive earthwork, dated between the 5th and 7th centuries, it may well mark the one-time limit of Wessex where the 10-mile eastern stretch runs through Wiltshire. It might have been a Romano-British defence against the Saxons or, more likely, a later Saxon point of division. This is one of a myriad of ancient earthworks on these hilltops. Along the way, our steps also pass **Adam's Grave**, a late Neolithic long barrow that is 200 ft long, 100 ft wide and 20 ft high. Excavations in the 19th century revealed several skeletons and a leaf arrowhead. This is said to be the site of a battle in AD 592 between the Saxons of Wessex and those of Ceawlin of the Upper Thames Valley. The *Anglo Saxon Chronicle* records a 'great slaughter' here, a far cry from the peaceful spot that Adam's Grave is today, set high on the hilltops with commanding views over the Pewsey Vale.

The **Pewsey Downs National Nature Reserve** lies on a steep south-facing scarp slope that runs along the northern side of the Vale of Pewsey. This is one of the largest downland sites now left free from the arable farmer's plough and fertiliser. The flora of this upland landscape draws botanists from far and wide, with species such as the burnt and bee orchid, the chalk milkwort, the bastard-toadflax and the field fleawort, all being residents of this protected environment. The reserve is also the home of the **Alton Barnes White Horse**, 650 ft above sea-level and said to be visible from Old Sarum near Salisbury, some 20 miles away. It was cut in 1812 at the expense of a Mr Robert Pile of Alton Barnes, who gave a journeyman painter £20 to carry out the task. John Thorpe, nicknamed Jack the Painter, was foolishly paid in advance. He promptly disappeared! He was later hanged for some unrecorded crime, leaving Pile the task of finishing the horse himself.

Westbury White Horse

On the Fringe

Admiring the view.

T his walk, over tracks and fieldpaths, embraces some of the most attractive downland in southern England, together with Wiltshire's oldest white horse, an Iron Age hillfort and a selection of stupendous views. The hilltop would make a fine spot for a picnic.

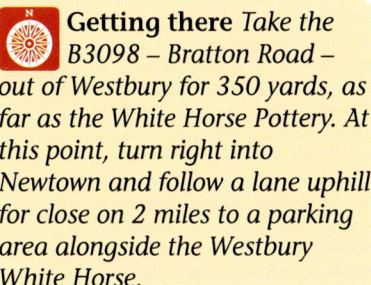

Getting there *Take the B3098 – Bratton Road – out of Westbury for 350 yards, as far as the White Horse Pottery. At this point, turn right into Newtown and follow a lane uphill for close on 2 miles to a parking area alongside the Westbury White Horse.*

Length of walk 2 miles.
Time 2 hours.
Terrain A walk on the relatively flat hilltops above the Westbury White Horse.

Start/Parking The free public car park adjacent to the Westbury White Horse (GR 899512).
Map OS Explorer 143 Warminster & Trowbridge.
Refreshments There are no refreshment facilities on this walk – why not take a picnic and supplement it with an ice-cream from the van that is often in the car park? Back in Westbury, there are several cafés and pubs.

1 Cross the road in front of the car park, pass through a

The Walk

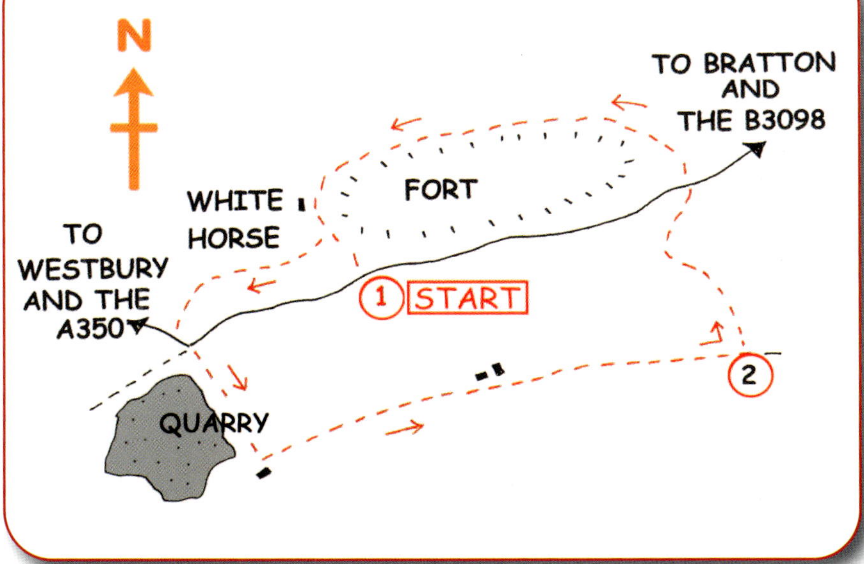

N

TO BRATTON
AND
THE B3098

WHITE
HORSE

FORT

TO
WESTBURY
AND THE
A350

1 START

2

QUARRY

handgate and follow a grassy path across to a pair of seats on the edge of the hilltop. Turn left and walk along the edge of the hilltop to a topograph before continuing along the path – it bears slightly left – to a stile in some bushes. Beyond this stile,

Taking a breather on Westbury Hill.

follow the line of a fence on the right across the hilltop. At the end of the field, pass through a gateway and continue ahead for 75 yards before turning left and walking uphill to a stile in the top field boundary. Join a road, turn left up to a junction and follow the track directly ahead that borders a quarry on the right. Continue up to an army checkpoint, turn left along the Imber Ranges Path and walk along to White Horse Farm. Continue along the track for another 350 yards to a bridleway on the left.

2 Follow this enclosed grassy track until it emerges onto open downland. At this point, keep on the path as it bears left and right before winding its way around the head of Combe Bottom. On reaching the road coming up to the hilltop from Bratton, turn right for a few paces before turning left to pass through a handgate. Follow a footpath to the left across to the ramparts of Bratton Fort. Follow the ramparts to the right along the edge of the hilltop and around to the Westbury White Horse. Beyond the horse, pass through a handgate and climb up to the open grassland crossed at the outset. Walk across to a gate and the road, and opposite is the car park.

◆ Fun Things to See and Do ◆

As with so many hilltop sites in Wiltshire, youngsters will enjoy their visit to the Westbury White Horse even more if they come armed with **a kite and a picnic**. There are also the ramparts of a hillfort – almost ubiquitous in these parts – where **ancient conflicts can be re-enacted**. It is always fascinating to **watch kite land-boarders**, who are often present here. In essence, these are lovers of extreme sports who use a specially designed kite to propel them across the hilltop on a skateboard … and on occasions the board and skater will lift a few feet into the air!

Kiddiwalks in Wiltshire

◆ Background Notes ◆

Combe Bottom – a striking landform along the way – is like a natural amphitheatre, a bowl in the landscape surrounded by unimproved chalk downland. Throughout the year, an abundance of plants adorn these hillsides – cowslip, vetch, trefoil, milkwort and scabious being typical downland species – whilst the turf is kept cropped and springy by the constant nibbling of sheep and lambs. This is a precious – but fast disappearing – habitat, with arable crops now being a more profitable commodity than lamb.

The **Westbury White Horse** was originally cut in AD 878 to commemorate Alfred's battle at Ethandun where the Danes were soundly defeated. Ethandun, incidentally, is widely thought to be nearby Edington. The original hill carving was allegedly 'a squat ungainly creature with a reptilian tail' that was not exactly held in high regard by the locals. In 1778, a Mr G. Gee – what an appropriate name – steward of the local landowner Lord Abingdon, remodelled the horse to today's distinctive design. For his efforts he was labelled an 'ignorant destroyer'.

Above and around the white horse is **Bratton Camp**, an Iron Age hillfort whose double bank and ditch enclose a site of some 25 acres. The views to the north from the ramparts are particularly extensive, and range from the Mendip Hills and the Cotswolds around to the Marlborough Downs and the Vale of Pewsey. It is immediately obvious why the site was ideal for such a construction, with any advancing enemy action being easily picked out across the vast swathes of countryside that lie at the foot of the downland escarpment. There would also be the not inconsiderable task for the attackers of having to scale the hilltop with arrows and other missiles flying down from above.

Shearwater

A Walk on the Wild Side

The firm track through the woodland.

Mention the Longleat Estate and most people would think of the grand mansion set in acres and acres of landscaped parkland, the safari park – of course – and the myriad attractions that include a tantalising maze and a miniature railway. The estate also extends to huge areas of woodland, a mixture of deciduous and coniferous trees that have the real feel of walking in a wilderness. Deep in the heart of the woodland lies Shearwater, a vast expanse of open water that is popular for both yachting and angling. It is also quite simply a beautiful lake that enjoys an enviable setting. This walk combines these two elements – the open water and the woodland – in what is a magnificent excursion into the great outdoors.

Kiddiwalks in Wiltshire

15

Length of walk 2 miles.
Time 2 hours.
Terrain Gently undulating paths through woodland. Be prepared for muddy patches following heavy rainfall.
Start/Parking Shearwater pay & display car park (GR 854420).
Map OS Explorer 143 Warminster & Trowbridge.

Refreshments The 15th-century Bargate Thatch teashop sits alongside the entrance to Shearwater. It serves all manner of snacks and soft drinks, as well as delicious cakes and cream teas.

1 Cross the road from the car park and follow the road that runs along the dam at the eastern end of Shearwater. Pass a sailing club and follow the road along to the left. Just on this bend, follow a track that heads off into the woodland beyond a barrier. Follow this track uphill for ¼ mile before continuing along the path as it assumes a level course. In

◆ Fun Things to See and Do ◆

Arrive at the right time and you might be fortunate enough to see **a carp** of up to 25 pounds in weight being lifted into some fisherman's keep-net … and that isn't the one that got away!

There are all manner of things to do in an area of woodland, such as that surrounding Shearwater Lake. At its simplest level, there is **wildlife spotting**. Bring some breadcrumbs or birdseed and scatter them twenty yards away from your hiding place … then just wait and watch and listen. There could be **capturing the enemy** – have one base guarded by an adult; the rest of the party has to try and creep up unseen and storm the base. Or it could just be a game of **hide-and-seek**, although given the dense nature of the woodland – and the complex footpath network – this is best played in a confined area!

The Walk

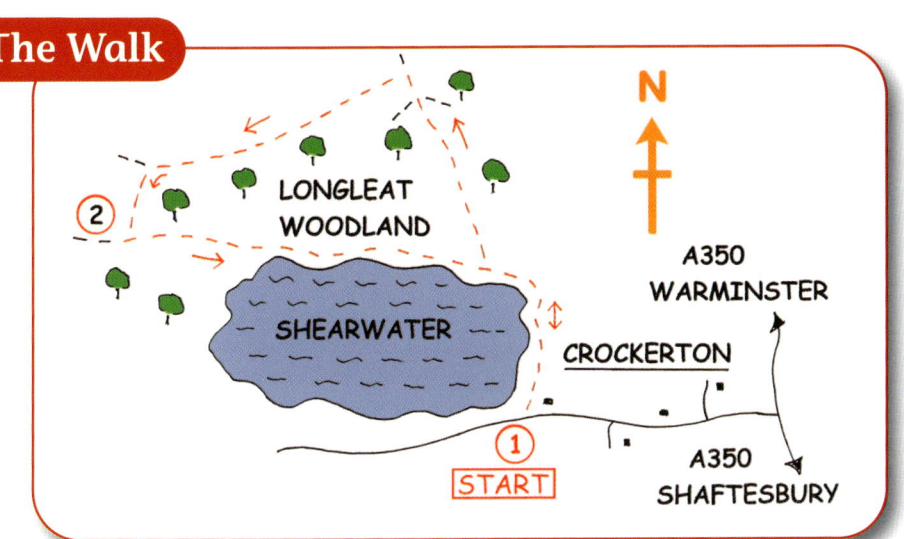

LONGLEAT
WOODLAND

②

N

A350
WARMINSTER

SHEARWATER

CROCKERTON

①

START

A350
SHAFTESBURY

200 yards, look out for a point where a track comes in on the right and two paths go off on the left. Take the second path on the left – it drops downhill and bears right – and continue for 350 yards to a distinct fork, ignoring earlier paths on the left.

② Veer left at this fork, dropping downhill, and keep on the main path ahead for 200 yards to a T-junction. Turn left along a track for 300 yards to another junction by a small pond. Turn left and follow a tarmac road to reach a barrier and Shearwater. Walk along the road beside the lake back to the sailing club and across the dam back to the car park.

The lake in tranquil mood.

Kiddiwalks in Wiltshire

15

◆ Background Notes ◆

Generations of families in West Wiltshire have enjoyed a pleasant few hours lazing and relaxing on the banks of **Shearwater Lake**. The 38 acres of open water, now part of the Longleat Estate, were designed in 1791 by Francis Drake of Bridgwater. Today, Shearwater is a popular location for both anglers and sailors, the surrounding mature trees and shrubs making this one of the most scenic recreational spots in southern Britain. The lake itself was created by damming a shallow valley that was fed by a pair of small streams. Rhododendrons grow around much of Shearwater, together with a range of broad-leaved trees that include beech, oak and elder. Surprisingly, the lake does not attract large numbers of water birds or a great variety of species. Mallard, coot and great crested grebe are permanent fixtures on the water, whilst mandarins, gadwalls and shovelers are but occasional visitors. Herons and kingfishers are also known to put in the occasional fleeting appearance.

Shearwater Lake is a **popular spot for anglers**, especially those seeking the magnificent carp. In Europe, even when not fished for food, these are eagerly sought out, being considered highly prized coarse fish that are both difficult to hook and to land. The UK has a thriving carp angling market and this has spawned a number of specialised publications such as *Advanced Carp Fishing* and *Total Carp*. The carp fishermen even seem to have adopted their own uniform, a form of army battle dress.

Around Shearwater lie **acres and acres of woodland**, consisting mainly of recently planted coniferous species interspersed with a number of more mature conifers. The sharp eye might well pick out the Douglas fir, for example, as well as sequoia and western red cedar, larch and Norway spruce. By contrast with the popular and often crowded banks of the lake, the woodland paths can be virtually deserted, even on a summer's weekend, making this an even better location for the ornithologist. Here the observant visitor might spot the sparrowhawk or buzzard, the kestrel or the tawny owl, as well as woodpeckers and tree creepers.

Stonehenge

The Imprint of the Ancients

Tourists heading for the Stones.

This walk allows the ancient monument of Stonehenge to be viewed from a distance, far away from the hustle-and-bustle of the tourist traffic. The paths are all within National Trust land, and are generally level and easy to negotiate. A number of other important archaeological sites can be seen along the way – the Cursus and the Cursus Barrows, the New King Barrows and the Avenue. This is a wander through the pages of ancient history in one of the most important areas for archaeological remains in the world.

16

Getting there *Leave the A303 west of Amesbury – signposted to Stonehenge – and follow the A344 towards Shrewton. Immediately past the Stonehenge car park, turn right and park on a broad track. The A344 east of Shrewton is also reached from the A360 south of Devizes.*

Length of walk 2¼ miles.
Time 2 hours.
Terrain A very gently undulating landscape around Stonehenge.
Start/Parking A broad track just to the west of the Stonehenge car park (GR 120423).

Map OS Explorer 130 Salisbury & Stonehenge.
Refreshments Drinks, light snacks and ice-creams are available at the Stonehenge site.

1 Follow the track away from the A344 for 600 yards to an information board describing the Cursus. Continue for another 20 yards before crossing a stile on the right. Walk across to the far left-hand corner of the field ahead, cross a stile alongside a gate and walk on for 100 yards to another gate and stile. Ahead, the broad open field is the course of the Cursus – walk

The Walk

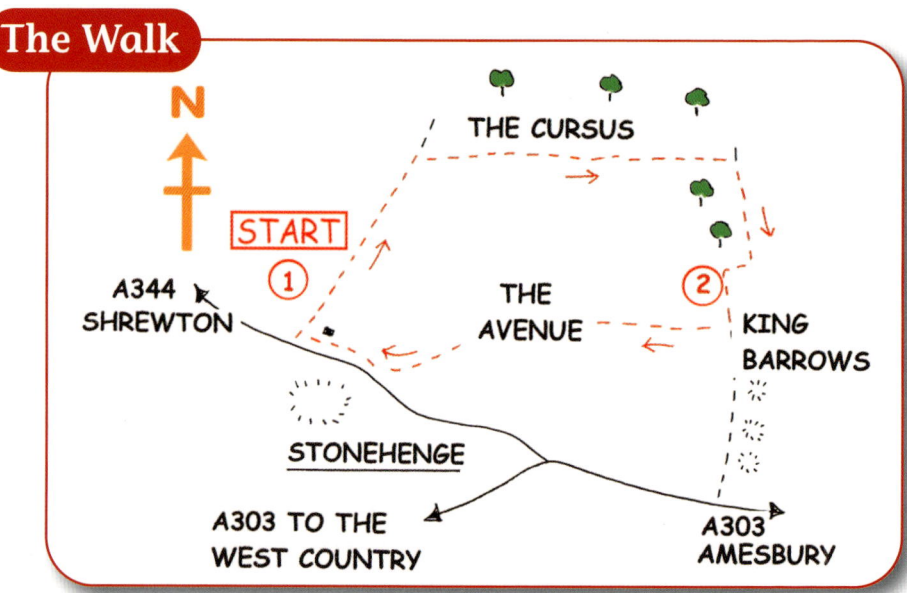

its whole length to a stile in the far-left hand corner, before continuing along a track to a junction. Turn right and, in 300 yards, turn right along a side track waymarked to the King Barrows. Follow the track down to a viewpoint on the King Barrows Ridge before bearing left.

◆ Fun Things to See and Do ◆

The **vast stones set in concentric circles** of Stonehenge date back thousands of years and present a mysterious feature on the landscape. Nearby lie **ancient burial chambers** – known as round barrows – that are equally haunting and intriguing.

If you decide to combine a visit to Stonehenge itself with the walk, you will find that English Heritage has developed a range of **fun activities relating to the site**. These include the archaeologist game, the dustbin and the skeleton game, all of which will add to the children's enjoyment. The link to the relevant page of the website is quite complex, so it is far easier to simply enter 'Children Stonehenge' into an internet search engine.

The Stonehenge area also offers a rich natural history. The very fortunate few might spot a **roe deer**. Hares are more common, whilst the **skylark** and the **partridge** both exist in large numbers. In the autumn months, large **flocks of peewits** will be seen feeding off of the stubble and recently ploughed land in the area.

Salisbury Plain is an area with a strong MOD presence. With the army base at Larkhill and Boscombe Down Airfield both within 3 miles of Stonehenge, many **military vehicles and planes** are likely to be seen on the roads and in the air around this most ancient of monuments.

2 In 200 yards, pass through a handgate on the right just before an information board; the Kings Barrows lie just a short distance along the track on the left. The walk now passes onto the course of the Avenue. Walk straight ahead across an open field, dropping down to a gate in the fence in a dip, initially hidden. Beyond this gate, walk across to an information board. Beyond this information board, walk uphill towards Stonehenge. On reaching a fence and the A344 alongside Stonehenge, turn right to a stile in the corner of the field. Continue through the car park to a gap in the fence at the end. This gap leads to the track where your vehicle is parked.

◆ Background Notes ◆

Stonehenge is a prehistoric monument of worldwide fame, dating from 2800 BC. Originally it was simply a henge monument consisting of a bank and external ditch. The concentric stone circles were a later addition. The stones are a mixture of sarsens from the nearby Marlborough Downs and bluestones from the Prescelly Hills in West Wales. This was undoubtedly a sacred site for ancient people, although speculation as to its precise function continues to this day. A vast body of literature has been written on Stonehenge, and for a more detailed treatment you can purchase one of the many booklets available at the site shop.

Around Stonehenge lie a number of equally mysterious and mystical monuments. The **King Barrows**, a collection of large round barrows, enjoy an atmospheric location within a beech wood. The setting is cool, dark and shadowy, and very much in keeping with the theme of ancient burial chambers. **The Avenue** would have provided a splendid approach to the Stonehenge site during ancient religious rituals, although little remains of this ceremonial walkway. **The Cursus**, a remarkable enclosure of two parallel banks and ditches some 100 yards apart, has equally puzzling origins to Stonehenge. Its length and level gradient does, however, lend credence to the view that this was used for horse or chariot racing.

White Sheet Hill

Big Sky Country

Model plane enthusiasts on White Sheet Hill.

S tourhead, the flagship National Trust property in South Wiltshire, is
most associated with the grand Palladian mansion and the nearby
ornamental gardens. What most visitors to the estate miss, however,
are the vast swathes of countryside that surround the tourist honeypot.
Round about are many hundreds of acres of ancient woodland and open
chalk downland, all lovingly cared for and tended by the National Trust.
White Sheet Hill provides a stunning backdrop to the Stourhead Estate,
its open hilltops bringing expansive views across towards the great house
and beyond to Alfred's Tower. This is big sky country, perfect for those
days when cumulus clouds drift across a blue summer sky.

Kiddiwalks in Wiltshire

17

Getting there *Take the B3092 between Frome and Mere. Immediately south of the Red Lion Inn at Kilmington (to the north of Stourhead), turn off eastwards along an unmarked lane. In 600 yards, where the lane becomes an unmetalled track, turn right into a parking area.*

Length of walk 2 miles.
Time 1½ hours.
Terrain Tracks and grassy paths on the downs.
Start/Parking White Sheet Hill free car park (GR 797350).

Map OS Explorers 142 Shepton Mallet & Mendip Hills East and 143 Warminster & Trowbridge.
Refreshments The lane to White Sheet Hill leaves the B3092 by the Red Lion Inn, an atmospheric country pub owned by the National Trust, offering good value traditional lunches and an attractive garden. White Sheet Hill would also make the perfect spot for a picnic.

① Leave the car park, turn right and follow a track uphill for just over ¼ mile to a point where the track begins to bear right. Pass

The Walk

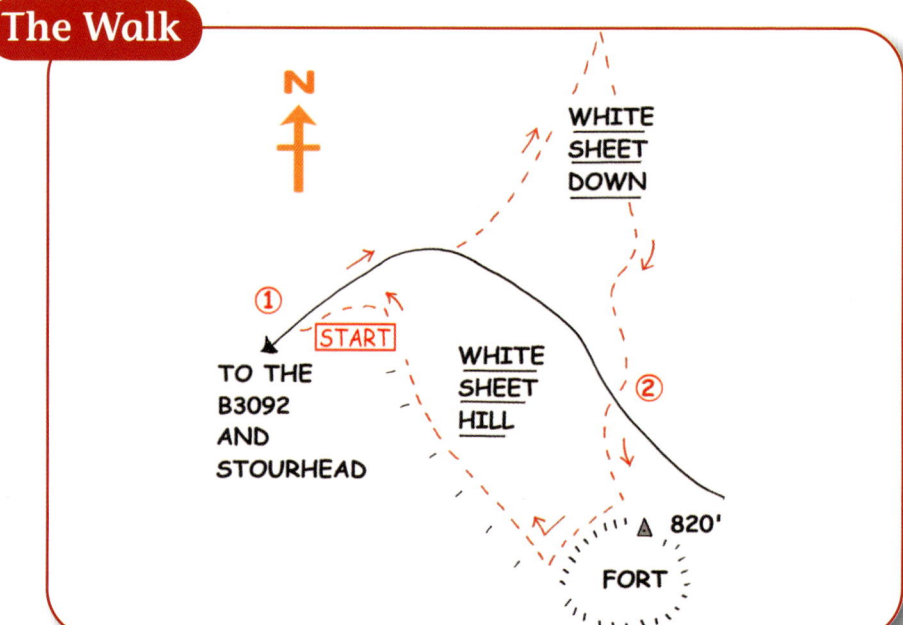

through a handgate and enter the National Trust's White Sheet Down property – there is a NT sign at this point. Follow the grassy path across the down for 600 yards to a point where the path drops downhill to reach an embankment on the left – a cross dyke. At this point, turn right and walk across the open grassland for a few paces to reach another grassy path. Follow this path to the right uphill and, where the path peters out, continue across the open grassland, passing above an impressive combe on the left. As another cross dyke approaches, turn right to reach a stile in the fence above this embankment.

2 Cross a track to a stile opposite – alongside a NT information board – and enter an open hilltop enclosure. Turn left, following a fence on the left, to reach the ramparts of a hillfort on what is White Sheet Hill. Follow the whole length of the first rampart down to the edge of the hilltop, leave the rampart and walk to the right across the edge of the hilltop. On the far side of the hilltop, having passed a section of cross dyke and walked below a round barrow, cross a stile in the fence. Follow a path around to the left and down some steps into an area of former chalk quarrying. Walk

◆ Fun Things to See and Do ◆

White Sheet Hill can offer all of the various types of activity that many hilltops in Wiltshire offer – a hillfort upon which to **re-enact ancient battles**, a wide range of **wild flowers and butterflies** to spot, excellent **kite-flying** and many places to enjoy a picnic. Unique to White Sheet Hill, however, is the **White Sheet Radio Flying Club**. Members of the club enjoy constructing and flying 'silent flight' model aircraft, more generally known as gliders. These members have a broad range of interests from thermal soaring to flying scale replicas. Visit the club's website to find out when the next 'scale day' is being held. On these days, large numbers of scale models can be seen circling around the hilltop.

down through the quarry and, 30 yards before the trees at the bottom of the slope, follow a path that bears left over to a fence on the edge of the hill. Follow this fence to the right down to a stile and the car park.

A trig point on the

◆ Background Notes ◆

White Sheet Hill, as well as being a fine viewpoint, is an archaeologist's dream. At the southern end is a hillfort, protected by a single bank and ditch on the steepest sides and three banks and ditches on the flatter north-eastern side. Across the middle of the hilltop runs a cross-ridge dyke, probably associated with the Iron Age hillfort, the function of which was to control the movement of livestock. At the northern end of the hill lies the site of a causewayed enclosure dating from 3000 BC.

The hilltop is now a National Trust property and is maintained as **unimproved chalk grassland**, where the plough and fertiliser are banned. The result is an abundance of flora in season, including the cowslip, orchids, vetches and campanulas, as well as butterflies, including the rare chalk-hill blue. As a concession to modern times, the hilltop is used by the local model aircraft club. At weekends, it is normal to find twenty or thirty enthusiasts flying their varied craft high above the downs. Incidentally, the National Trust holds an annual 'Kite Day' on White Sheet Hill each year, too. This is usually in June, and is a spectacular and colourful occasion on this open hilltop site.

The track that takes the walk from the car park onto the hilltop is an **ancient route from Salisbury to the West Country**. Alongside the track, a milestone erected in 1752 records that we are 'XXIII miles from Sarum'.

Wardour

Exploring Two Castles – Old and New

The ruins of Old Wardour.

Deep in the South Wiltshire countryside, amidst an undulating landscape bounded by wooded slopes, lie Old and New Wardour Castles. New Wardour Castle does not immediately have that castle feel, being a Palladian mansion dating from the second half of the 18th century. Old Wardour has the real castle atmosphere – it's a romantic ruin with towers and battlements that would make a perfect film set. In fact, part of Robin Hood – Prince of Thieves was filmed here. Woodland tracks, fieldpaths and quiet lanes connect this pair of historic buildings, making for a peaceful walk in a remote setting, seemingly a million years away from the bloodshed and violence that took place here when the castle was ransacked during the English Civil War.

Kiddiwalks in Wiltshire

18

Getting there *Old Wardour Castle is signposted from the A350, 2 miles north of Shaftesbury. The castle is also signposted from the A30, 2 miles south-west of Tisbury. A cul de sac lane leads down to a car park alongside the castle.*

Length of walk 2½ miles.
Time 2 hours.
Terrain An undulating landscape in the heart of South Wiltshire. There may be some mud on the woodland paths following heavy rainfall.
Start/Parking The free car park at Old Wardour Castle (GR 938263).

Map OS Explorer 118 Shaftesbury & Cranborne Chase.
Refreshments These are available at Old Wardour Castle, where there is also a picnic area.

1 From the car park, follow the path up towards the entrance to the castle. Where the path bears right to the entrance kiosk, keep walking ahead along a footpath that enters woodland. In 100 yards, at a fork, veer left and follow a path that climbs uphill through the woodland, shortly passing underneath a bridge. At a junction at the top of the woodland, ignore the path to

◆ Fun Things to See and Do ◆

Old Wardour Castle is just what children would expect of a castle – battlements and towers and in a ruinous state following bitter fighting and warfare. **Exploring the ruin** will bring alive those violent days when Englishman fought Englishman in the Civil War of the 1640s.

A range of **special events** is held at Old Wardour Castle each year. These might typically include medieval falconry, traditional games and haunted tours, as well as a Christmas trail for children. For further information visit the castle's website, found on www.english-heritage.org.uk

The Walk

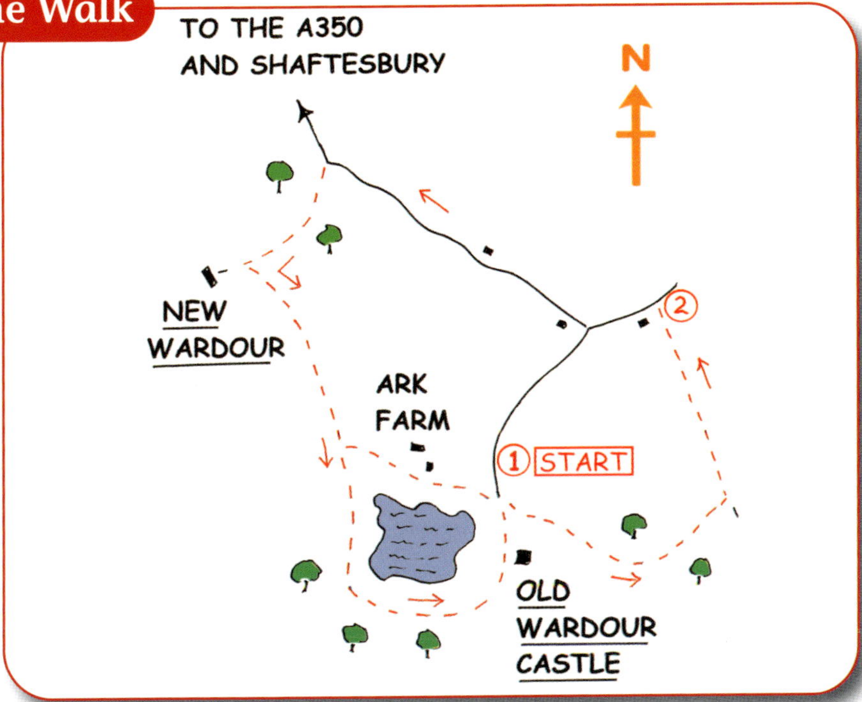

TO THE A350
AND SHAFTESBURY

N

NEW
WARDOUR

ARK
FARM

① START

②

OLD
WARDOUR
CASTLE

the right, keeping ahead along
an enclosed path that crosses
an open hilltop. On the far side
of the hilltop, enter some
woodland and, in 20 yards,
turn left along a prominent
track marked as a restricted
byway. Follow this track for
½ mile until it reaches a quiet
country lane.

❷ Turn left and follow this
lane for ½ mile to a footpath on
the left on a right-hand bend.
Turn left at this point – passing

Cowslips.

The view from the battlements of Old Wardour Castle.

through a gap in a wooden fence – and follow the path as it bears right to pass through bushes before emerging onto a track just before the lawns in front of New Wardour Castle. *Detour to explore* the New Wardour Castle site. *For the main walk,* turn left along this track and, in 20 yards, turn left to a gate and stile. Beyond the stile, follow a slightly sunken grassy path across an open field in the direction of Ark

Farm. In ¼ mile, on the far side of the field, cross a stile and follow a track ahead for 300 yards to a junction in front of an area of woodland.

Turn left and follow a path for 300 yards to the boundary wall of Old Wardour Castle. Keep left and walk around to the car park.

◆ Background Notes ◆

Old Wardour Castle was originally built in the 14th century for John, 5th Lord Lovel of Tichmarsh, and remodelled in the 16th century. The castle enjoys a fine location on rising wooded ground above a lake – Cresswell's Pond – an austere and impressive relic from a bygone age. Substantially updated by the staunchly Roman Catholic Arundell family after 1570, the castle saw much fighting during the Civil War. In 1643 the 60-year-old Lady Arundell was forced to surrender it to Parliament. But the new garrison was almost immediately besieged in turn by Royalist forces led by her son. After an eventful 10 months of bombardment and undermining, they finally capitulated in March 1644. The badly damaged castle became a romantic ruin located around its hexagonal courtyard. In the 18th century it was incorporated into the landscaped grounds of Lord Arundell's New Wardour Castle.

New Wardour Castle, which is the largest Georgian house in Wiltshire, is described as ashlar-faced and stern by the architectural historian, Sir Nikolaus Pevsner. To quote the architectural detail, the house consists of a main block, nine windows wide, and quadrant links of five windows to three-bay pavilions. The property includes a Roman Catholic chapel known as All Saints, Wardour, expanded by John Soane in 1788 on instruction from the 8th Lord Arundell of Wardour. It still has regular Sunday services and is occasionally used for musical events. Following the death of the last Lord Arundell in 1944, the house became the home of Cranbourne Chase School. Following the school's closure in 1990, the house was converted into a series of luxury apartments.

Fovant

Badges of Glory

The badges seen from below the hillside.

The county of Wiltshire is renowned for its chalk hill-figures, in particular the large number of white horses such as those at Cherhill and Westbury. This walk features an unusual group of military badges carved on the downland escarpment above Fovant. The village lies in the south of the county, a few miles west of Salisbury, but the landscape is a familiar one of chalk downs and clay vale. The walk itself is short, with the climb onto the downland hilltop being its only strenuous feature, but the rewards are worthwhile in terms of expansive views, a rich downland flora, an ancient hillfort and the opportunity to examine those badges close up.

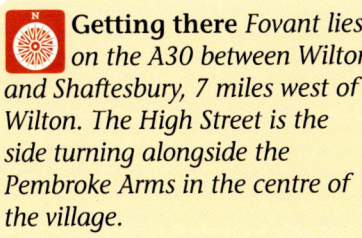

Getting there *Fovant lies on the A30 between Wilton and Shaftesbury, 7 miles west of Wilton. The High Street is the side turning alongside the Pembroke Arms in the centre of the village.*

Length of walk 2 miles.
Time 1½ hours.
Terrain Tracks and grassy downland paths.

Start/Parking Fovant's High Street alongside the Pembroke Arms (GR 007285).
Map OS Explorer 130 Salisbury & Stonehenge.
Refreshments Fovant Down is a glorious spot for a picnic – so come well prepared. Alternatively, the creeper-covered Pembroke Arms has an excellent garden that welcomes families.

◆ Fun Things to See and Do ◆

The hilltops above Fovant provide a host of things to see and do. **Bring along a kite** and you will have great fun as it soars high above Fovant Down. There are also the remains of an ancient hillfort, whose gentle ramparts provide a safe environment for children to **re-enact ancient battles**. If you have a spotter's guide to **wild flowers** with you, the children will soon (in season) be identifying cowslips and primroses, scabious and trefoil, as well as a number of wild orchids.

Chalk hill-figures were created by drawing an outline of a horse or – in this case – military badges onto the hillside grasses. The topsoil was then dug away and the resulting 'hole' filled in with chalk. The children should be able to **spot eight badges** on the hillside, as well as identifying to which regiment each one belonged. A few clues – the Royal Wiltshire Yeomanry badge displays the initials RWY whilst in the case of the City of London Regiment it is CLR. There is also the Royal Corps of Signal with a figure supporting a crown, as well as the Devonshire Regiment with its prominent star.

The Walk

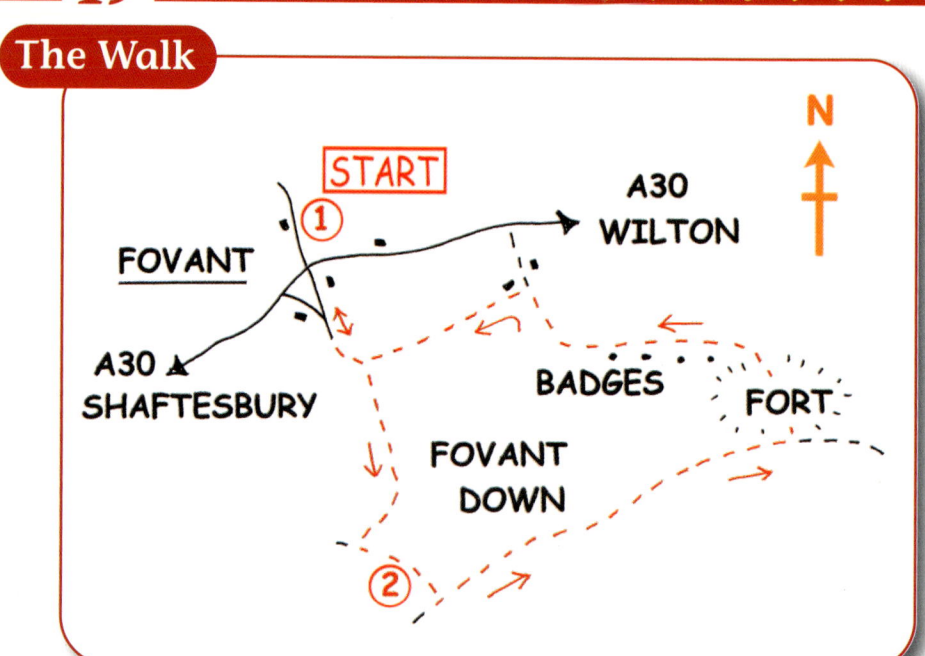

START

A30 WILTON

FOVANT

A30 SHAFTESBURY

BADGES

FORT

FOVANT DOWN

N

1 Walk back to the A30 and follow Brook Street, the road opposite slightly to the right. At the end of Brook Street, where it bears right back to the main road, keep ahead along an unmetalled road that winds its way between a number of properties. Where this track bears left by open fields, pass through a gate on the right and follow a bridleway along the left edges of two fields towards the downland escarpment. In the corner of the field immediately below the escarpment, bear left to a handgate before following a flat grassy path to the right to a junction almost on the hilltop. At this junction, turn left and follow a path for 200 yards to a broad gravelled track.

2 Follow this track to the left for just over ½ mile to a stile and footpath on the left, just before a right-hand bend with a fine view across the downs on the right. Walk across to the ramparts of Chiselbury Fort. Follow the ramparts, on the left, around to the northern side of the fort, high above Fovant.

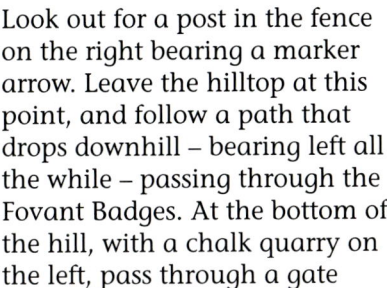

Look out for a post in the fence on the right bearing a marker arrow. Leave the hilltop at this point, and follow a path that drops downhill – bearing left all the while – passing through the Fovant Badges. At the bottom of the hill, with a chalk quarry on the left, pass through a gate on the right and walk down to East Farm. At a junction by the farm, follow a track to the left for 300 yards at which point the track bears right back down to Brook Street. Retrace your steps along Brook Street to the A30, before crossing over to the High Street.

◆ Background Notes ◆

The **Fovant Badges** are carved on the steep north-western slopes of Fovant Down. During the First World War, many troops were billeted at training camps in the locality before seeing action on the Western Front. Volunteers would work on the emblems in the early morning, with each design taking several months to complete. The London Rifle Brigade thought up the idea of the badges, and theirs was the first to be cut. The other badges include those of the Royal Wiltshire Yeomanry, the Sixth London Rifles and the Royal Warwickshire Yeomanry. The collection is certainly impressive, and many a motorist on the A30 must have been distracted from the road ahead by this most unusual of sights. The Fovant Badges Society has an excellent website whose address is www.fovantbadges.com and the site documents all of the badges still in situ on Fovant Down, as well as those that have been lost over the years.

On the hilltop above the badges lie the remains of a much earlier military occupation, **Chiselbury Camp**. This is an Iron Age hillfort dating from about 200 BC, consisting of a single bank, with double ramparts on the south-western side. The enclosure extends to some nine acres. At over 650 ft above sea-level, and sited atop a steep escarpment, the camp provides an excellent viewpoint overlooking the Nadder Valley below. Given the commanding views from the site, and the protection afforded by a steep hillside slope, it is obvious why this site was chosen for such a settlement.

Old Sarum

The Abandoned City

The site of the old cathedral.

From the banks of the River Avon, a gently flowing chalk stream, this walk climbs onto a hilltop site that has been the subject of multi-occupancy over many centuries. Old Sarum was the original site of the City of Salisbury, but was abandoned in 1331, a tale that is related below. The present-day city is never far away, but you will enjoy beautiful views of the Avon and its neighbouring meadows as you go. This is truly a walk back through the pages of history.

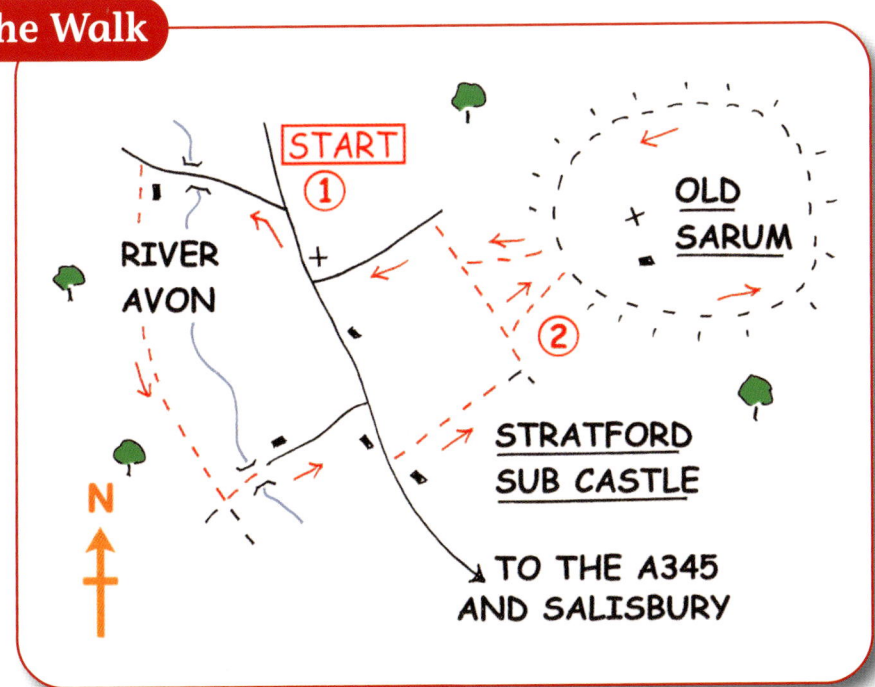

Getting there *Follow the A345 north from the A36 in Salisbury for just 200 yards before taking a left turn to Stratford sub Castle. Park on the roadside by the church in 1 mile.*

Length of walk 2½ miles.
Time 2 hours.
Terrain Tracks and grassy paths.
Start/Parking Stratford sub Castle church (GR 130327).
Map OS Explorer 130 Salisbury & Stonehenge.

Refreshments There are refreshment facilities at the Old Sarum site, which is also an excellent spot for a picnic.

1 Facing Stratford sub Castle church, follow the road to the left along to a junction by the River Avon. Keep left, crossing the river, and walk along the road for 350 yards to a bend by Avon Farm. Turn left and follow a footpath that runs along the right-hand side of the converted farm buildings before entering an open

The Walk

START
①
RIVER AVON
OLD SARUM
②
STRATFORD SUB CASTLE
TO THE A345 AND SALISBURY
N

field. Take the path along the left edge of this field to a stile and handgate, before continuing along an enclosed path for 600 yards to a point where a tarmac path crosses the footpath. Turn left, following the path down to the Avon and onto a lane. Continue along this lane to its junction with the road in Stratford sub Castle. Turn right and, in 200 yards, just past a property called Little Thatches on the right, turn left onto a

bridleway that climbs uphill towards Old Sarum.

2 At a junction on the hilltop just below the castle, turn left and follow a path along the hillside below Old Sarum. In 100 yards, pass through a gate on the right and take a path that climbs uphill to reach the outer rampart of Old Sarum. Follow this rampart to the right all the way around to the entrance road leading into the castle site. Walk

◆ Fun Things to See and Do ◆

The **vast ramparts** at Old Sarum have been played on and enjoyed by countless generations of youngsters. This is the perfect place to re-enact battles from centuries past, although care will be needed on the outer ramparts with their very steep gradients. At the site, it is also possible to visit the **ruins of the old Norman castle**, with its ancient stone walls and narrow sloping stairways.

Alfred Watkins in his book *The Old Straight Track* noted how many ancient monuments are aligned on straight lines. There is no known reason why this should be, making these '**ley lines**' rather mysterious and puzzling features of our landscape. Older children might be interested in drawing a line on a map –the scale of the OS Landranger 184 would be just right – from Old Sarum to Salisbury Cathedral. If this line is extended to the north and south they can see how many other ancient features lie on its course.

along this road up to a car park just past the inner rampart. Turn right to reach a stile on the right and climb onto the inner rampart. Follow this rampart to the left all the way around to the southern end of the remains of a cathedral. Just beyond this point, follow a sunken path on the right that drops down to the outer rampart. On reaching this rampart, high above Stratford sub Castle, turn left. In a few paces, veer right onto a path that drops down the hillside to a handgate and enclosed path. Follow this path to the right to a junction with a byway in 100 yards. Turn left and walk on this byway down to its junction with the road in Stratford sub Castle. Turn right to return to the church.

Imaginative topiary outside the church in Stratford sub Castle.

Kiddiwalks in Wiltshire

20

◆ Background Notes ◆

Old Sarum is a site that has been occupied by just about every conceivable wave of settlers down through the ages. Iron Age settlers constructed the massive outer ramparts and ditches, and subsequently the Romans, the Saxons, the Danes and the Normans each in turn occupied the site and left their mark. In the 11th century the Normans built both a cathedral and a castle on this hilltop site. The soldiers proved such disagreeable neighbours for the clergy that, in 1331, the cathedral was abandoned and its materials moved to the site of New Sarum – modern Salisbury – where it was rebuilt. The outer ramparts and the ground plan of the cathedral are open freely at all times, whilst the remains of the castle within the inner ring can be viewed for a modest admission charge (for details see the English Heritage website).

One landmark that you cannot miss on this walk is **Salisbury Cathedral,** just over one mile south of Old Sarum. The 404 ft spire is the tallest in England, and completely dominates the city's skyline. In the capstone of the spire is a tiny lead box with a fragment of woven fabric, put there in 1375. It is supposedly a relic of the Virgin that will guard the spire from lightning and all harm.